How to be a Storyteller

Essays and Advice on the Art of Storytelling

K. Sean Buvala, Editor

© 2012 by K. Sean Buvala.

Published by:
Creation Company Consultants
PO Box 392 Tolleson, AZ USA 85353
http://www.howtobeastoryteller
sean@storyteller.net
Twitter: @storyteller

ISBN: 978-1481091121

Please note: The authors and publisher have strived to be as accurate and complete as possible in the creation of this book. While all attempts have been made to verify information provided in this publication, the authors and publisher assume no responsibility for errors, omissions, or contrary interpretation of the subject matter herein. Any perceived slights of specific persons, peoples, or organizations are unintentional. Readers should rely on their own judgment about their individual circumstances to act accordingly. This book is not for use as a source of specific legal, business, accounting, medical or financial advice for any individual. This book is intended for the entertainment and enrichment of our readers.

Acknowledgements

Thank you to all the contributors to this book. Our authors wrote their essays and advice to you motivated by their love of the storytelling art form. We are grateful for their participation in this 15th-anniversary project from Storyteller.net.

Please visit Storyteller.net for even more articles, stories and resources.

Table of Contents

Storytelling is an art form.

Diversity: Read This First

Author: K. Sean Buvala

Diversity.

When I first set out to create this "How to be a Storyteller" compilation book, I knew that I'd receive original and interesting chapters. However, even I, after storytelling since 1986, was surprised at the diversity of contributions I received.

There was a diversity of opinions, even on the same topics within different articles. This was a diversity that I did not expect. I thought, "Don't 'all' storytellers have the same opinions on some of the basic construction of a story?" No, they do not and did not and I have learned even more about what makes up a storyteller.

There was a diversity of writing styles. While I expected that the authors would all bring their own "voice" to their chapters, I was surprised at the range of voices. With some storytellers their writing was very organized and even academic. With others, they wrote as if they were telling wild and fun stories to the reader. In editing, I've kept much of those voices even if it resulted in some "unusual" editing choices. I hope that as you read each chapter, you appreciate the unique gift from each author. I think that every chapter is like its own theme-park ride with some running up and down, back and forth while others run a bit more leisurely.

There was a diversity of subjects. When I set out the open call for chapter submissions, I went to the storytellers listed in the Storyteller.net directory. I thought

I might have to choose among authors who all would submit chapters on the same limited subjects. Rather than that, I received a very diverse range of topics. Do you want the basics of storytelling around campfires? We have that. There is a chapter on the latest trend for storytelling at "slam" events. We have chapters about basic storytelling and some chapters on a wide variety of subjects ranging from advanced techniques to cross-cultural translation to courtroom storytelling. You will read both reflections and practical advice. I have tried to mix the expected with the unexpected in this book.

I did expect the diversity of geographical locations. Storyteller.net, now in its 15th year of service as of this writing in 2012, has always hosted storytellers, via our directory and articles, from all over the world. You will find the locations of the authors to be an international mix.

This is a very broad collection of articles. So with all that in mind, how might you use this book?

Just to be clear, this book is about the art and techniques of oral storytelling. If you are looking for advice on writing stories or presenting them through digital or other non-verbal means, this book will not teach you any of that specifically. I know that everyone benefits by the skill and talent of oral storytelling. If you are communicating with others, oral storytelling will always be the foundation with which you must begin.

While the book does stand together as a whole, each chapter can be read as its own individual educational tool. The only "order" of the articles is that I tried to place the more family-oriented articles together followed by the more adult-focused parts. With that in mind, feel free to jump around in your reading, starting with the subjects that interest you the most, then moving towards those sections whose subjects might surprise or challenge you.

It might be fun to go at this book with a group. For example, storytelling guilds will find it interesting to tackle a chapter at each meeting, finding points of agreement or disagreement with the authors. Then, through discussion of the topic, learn more with other guild members.

This book can also be a catalyst for your own development as an individual. I'd suggest reading the book with note-taking materials handy. Write about what each chapter teaches, affirms or challenges you in your own storytelling and public speaking. Write about how the chapters might help you form your own philosophy of storytelling.

We want to know what you think about the book. Join us for a discussion or come learn more about the contributors, many having posted web-only comments about their subjects, when you visit our website at http://www.howtobeastoryteller.com .

Thanks for joining us in this project. My thanks to Michelle Buvala for many hours of editing work on the chapters in this book.

-K. Sean Buvala, Editor.

About the Author:

Sean Buvala has been working with storytelling and communication since 1986. He started his work by accidentally using active storytelling to convert a classroom of slightly homicidal 8th-grade teenagers from angry kids to storytelling practitioners. From then on, both the kids and Sean were sold on the influence of great and fun stories.

From kids in classrooms to bosses in boardrooms, from presenting workshops for global salt miners to consulting with Ph.D.'s in pharmaceuticals, Sean teaches and tells stories in nearly every industry and setting. Along the way, there has been some award-recognition and the authoring of a growing pile of books, articles, audios and videos. He makes his home in Arizona with four daughters and one wife.

Find his website at:
http://www.seantells.com
or you can Twitter him @Storyteller.

How to be a Storyteller- An Introduction

Author: Dr. Margaret Read MacDonald

Don't worry. You already are a storyteller! Every time you tell someone about the remarkable thing that happened to you on the way to work today. . .you are telling a story. And you may have noticed that when you retell this story to another person. . .and then to another person. . .the story begins to get better? You automatically are shaping the story for best effect. This is the way that fish you caught gets bigger and bigger with each telling. You are creating a good story through retelling it. This is exactly the same technique that will serve you well when you tackle new material as a storyteller.

So how do you get started as a storyteller? First, you need to find a story that really excites you. Just any story will not do. To find that story, you will need to listen to many tellers and read through many story collections. It should be the story itself that inspires you to tell. When you see the right story you will know it. The tale should make you jump up and cry, "I can't wait to tell this story!"

Once you have found that story, identify your audience. Who can you "not wait" to tell it to? Plan a time to share the tale. Then get to work preparing your telling.

I suggest a one-hour lock-down session for story learning. Lock yourself in a room for total privacy. Turn off the television. Turn off your cell phone. Put out the dog and cat. Put someone else in charge of the kids.

Stand to do your story work. Research has shown that we learn 18% more when we are on our feet! Move around as you work on the story. Keep the blood flowing to your brain.

The easiest way to learn a story is to hear someone else tell it first. Since this is not always possible, you must perform it for yourself. Read the story aloud. Listen to your words. Read it aloud again and work on oral interpretation. Where will you raise your voice, speak more softly, speed up or slow down your pace? Which words will you stress?

Plan a few key points for your telling. Decide on a first and last sentence. These can be as simple as "Once upon a time" and "They lived happily ever after." The first and last sentences are the magical moments when you enter the world of story. You must know exactly what you want to say at these points. However, don't memorize the entire story. Just simply tell what happened in the tale. If there are beautiful phrases you especially want to keep, take a look at those and try to place them in your telling. If there are chants or songs within the story, you will need to memorize those. For the rest of the tale, just tell what happened.

Now put your book down and tell the tale. There is no right way to tell a story. Any way you tell it is just fine. Your audience has no idea how the story goes. So, if you forget part of the story that is no problem. You can always say something like "By the way, there was a dog coming down the road there, too." Professional storytellers do this all the time when they forget a detail. No one thinks a thing about it, since the professional storytellers obviously know what they are doing. The trick is to make the audience think you know what you are doing!

If you need to check back with your text at this point in your practice, do so.

Now try once more to tell the whole tale from start to finish. Try to get through without looking at your text. Keep at it until you have the tale in your head.

Over the next few days let the story percolate in your mind. Go over it again from time to time. Tell it to yourself while showering in the morning, or while taking the dog for a walk. Be sure you can tell your way through the entire tale.

Now you are finally ready to share your new story with an audience.

What about "storytelling techniques?" Forget about technique. Just relax and be yourself. The way you tell the story is the right way.

If you want to share specific literary tales as they are written, then it is true that you need to memorize them word for word. But if you are telling personal stories, they are yours to tell the way you want. If you are telling folktales, you are one of the folk. Folk stories change every time someone tells them. Now the tale has fallen into your hands, and you can deal with it as you wish.

As for style when you are telling to a live audience, know that some tellers stand while telling and some sit. Some leap about the stage. Some fold their hands and barely move a muscle. Within folk cultures these same variations exist. The thing that matters is the story. Can you convey it? Can you pass it along? Then do this in the style that feels most comfortable to you.

Now comes the storytelling event. Remember that the storytelling event is all about the audience. You are merely the facilitator who happens to have a story inside. Your thoughts should be entirely for your audience.

Storytelling is a nurturing act. You are caring for the audience, passing story to them. If, in your telling, even for a moment, you think about yourself with questions such as, "How am I sounding? How am I looking?" your mind is not in the right place. Your thoughts should all be for your listeners. "Are they understanding? How is the story coming across?"

When it is time to begin telling, gather your audience with your eyes. Make sure you can see all of their eyes.

Create a pregnant pause at the start of your telling. Start with a strong opening sentence. Speak it as if you mean business. Bring the audience right into the story with your own self-assurance. Once you have gathered them up and dropped them into the tale, they will relax as they know that they are in good hands. Now you can relax and just tell them what happened as the story goes along.

As you tell, watch your audience to make sure they are all following along. If one segment of the audience is restless, address yourself directly to them for a moment. However, keep your eyes roaming to pull in the entire group with your story energy. Let your hands be free to make natural gestures. Don't pre-plan gestures, just let your hands do what they normally want to do. Do not hide them in your pockets.

8

Close the story with even more self-assurance and a pre-rehearsed closing line. Stand at rest for a moment and let your audience come gradually back to the real world. They have been in a magical space. Let them return to reality at their own pace before you move on.

I like to think of the storytelling event as similar to a game teachers used to play in gym class. Students were given a huge balloon which they had to toss into the air together. Then each student had to keep running around and poking up at the balloon to keep it from hitting the ground.

Your audience is like that balloon. With the first sentence of your story, you push them up into the world of imagination. Now you must keep tapping them here and there, looking into all of their eyes, making sure no one is sinking toward the ground. Keep them all aloft in the world of your story. Then at the end, you stand back and let that balloon settle gently to the ground. Only then is the story finished.

A very important part of your storywork comes after the story is finished. Take time to think over the story event. What went really well? What would you change next time? Keep a story notebook and record this. For example, I know of a storyteller who has a little notebook with records of all the storytelling events she has offered. She lists the stories she told, how the telling went, what to keep and what to change next time. And when she is invited back to a school, she has all the info from her past visit right there!

Here is some very useful advice. Make an audio recording of your story as you are telling it. It doesn't have to be your most stunning telling and the recording does not need to be flawless. But six months later, when you want to tell that story again, you can just listen to the audio and hear exactly how you shaped the story last time. You don't have to begin from scratch with the tale text again. And if you do this faithfully, after a while you will have a great audio repertoire to fall back on, showing just how you have shaped these tales in the past.

Now just one more thing you need to do to become a storyteller. TELL STORIES!

About the Author:

Dr. Margaret Read MacDonald is the author of over 60 books on storytelling and folklore topics, drawing on her Folklore Ph.D. from Indiana University and her more than 30 years of service as a children's librarian. Retired now, she travels the world teaching storytelling and sharing tales in schools, libraries, and festivals. She is the author of "Peace Tales: World Folktales to Talk About" and "Teaching with Story" with Jennifer MacDonald Whitman and Nathaniel Whitman.

You can find her website by visiting:
http://www.margaretreadmacdonald.com.

How to be a Storyteller For Children

Author: John Weaver

The world needs more storytellers. Children and families need to be exposed to the art of storytelling. Yet many people don't even know storytellers exist. So there is room in the world for more of us, and I'm happy to be able to share with you a little bit of what it takes to be a storyteller for young audiences and their families.

First Things First

Do you even like children? This is the horse before which we must not put the cart. I have one favor to ask right now: if you do not like children, please do not endeavor to become a teacher or entertainer for this age group! It won't go well. As someone who has the occasional opportunity to book programs for family audiences, I have ended up in the past with entertainers who seemed unhappy with their lot. They were cranky, and in short, wanting to be in any other place than in front of a bunch of kids. So, if you and kids are a poor fit, please rethink this whole avenue of storytelling for children. Storytelling for adults is a very special field all in its own and perhaps that would be just right for you.

Now, if you want to work with this group, let me suggest something: don't talk down to them. Even though you hear it out of the mouths of wonderful people, the sing-songy, cloying tone of voice is not what's called for here. Respect your audience by not speaking down to them. You can speak simply, and for the appropriate age level, without ever resorting to baby talk.

On the topic of appropriateness to age level, I actually recommend that if it is at all possible for you, try to squeeze in a few courses in early-childhood development. Take as many as you can. Some colleges offer specific programs to teach storytelling and drama. Those could also be very beneficial, but what I'm talking about here is a course of study dedicated toward understanding and working with young children and their families. Within that curriculum there are courses related to literature for young children, which explains some things that work for young people, and why. I think that a broad study of early childhood (which covers birth through age 8) will help you tailor both your material and your interactions, giving your audience a product which is just right for them.

Find Your Story

Now it's time to find your story and get it straight. What kind of stories do you want to tell? Personal stories? Original tall tales? Classic folktales? Will you offer a mix of all of the above or something entirely different? It helps to first know your purpose in telling for young audiences. You may have a specific message you want to convey. Maybe you just have the desire to entertain. Perhaps you want to do both. It also helps to have an age range in mind. However, in practice, you will see that what you think is going to happen doesn't always quite work out the way you imagined! Keep this in mind always because I'm going to keep bringing it up: build flexibility into all of your plans.

If folktales are your interest, visit the libraries in your area and discover where those stories are shelved.

You should be able to find many instances where one story is represented in multiple books by multiple authors and illustrators. These old tales grew and spread in the imaginations of generations of storytellers and story listeners well before the dawn of publishing. When you find a story you like, read every version of it you can. Explore even more versions online. When you see what the common elements of the story are throughout its history, then you can rebuild it, adding the elements that are yours and yours alone.

If you are writing your own story or even, for that matter, adapting folklore, keep your audience in mind. A clear, easy-to-follow narrative is best. Take time to develop a structure your listeners can follow.

After you have put together enough stories for a session, develop an extra session's worth. Develop programming for several sessions. You want to be prepared to change your story in an unforeseen circumstance. You don't want to get bored with your stories. You want to be able to come back and share more stories with each group. Be prepared. Read more.

This all sounds like a lot of reading, doesn't it? It is! Keep reading. Never stop reading. Don't just read storybooks. Feed yourself regularly with news, and information, and literature, because anything that broadens your mind and feeds your imagination can also broaden and feed your performance.

Memorize your stories but not too well. For the beginning storyteller, the biggest fear can be that you'll forget your story. Experiment with different methods for learning your stories, and find the ways that work best for you. You could commit your tale to memory by hand writing and rewriting the whole thing over and over again.

The first time or two I took on storytelling, I did that handwriting process. However, I don't anymore. Another method I used in those initial days was to record myself, and listen to the recording repeatedly as I drove about in my car. I'd listen and re-listen to certain segments, to make sure I had them down right. I do not do that anymore.

I don't want to suggest you cannot use the full writing and recording methods. My primary message to you is to find your way using the methods that fit best with your own style. Here's the thing you need to know: I don't want you to get stuck in the trap of memorizing your story word-for-word. Your storytelling is not a recital. Storytelling is a living, breathing art. If you commit the important details of the story to memory, rather than the exact order of the exact words you've chosen, you allow the character and your imagination some room to play.

Try getting your stories secure in your mind by sketching or diagramming them. Emphasize the important plot points and your favorite lines of dialogue. This method can help you develop your story more. This dissection of the plot and action helps lay bare how the different elements fit together, and gives you an open opportunity to experiment with different actions and lines that may end up making your story even better. Further, going back over a brief list of the major plot elements of your story can be a great way to refresh your memory as you prepare for a performance. It can also help you to choose great story pairings, as you see complimentary elements pointed out in your notes.

Time to Perform

Once you've found your story, find your voice and the voice of everyone in your story, too. Vocal variation is an important part of engaging your audience of children. Pace, tone and volume need to keep up with the dramatic tension of the story itself. It all helps you pull in the "big fish" of the audience's interest!

Give your characters a little extra character by experimenting with different voices. It can be as subtle as a mild rise or drop in your pitch. You might try going the cartoon route, to give certain characters- perhaps and especially animals- a little something extra. Children will express surprise and delight in hearing such sounds coming from a grown person's mouth. You will have their attention. Remember these two things: make sure that no matter how "funny" the character's voice, it can still be understood. Don't hurt your throat and voice. Vocal stunts can hurt the vocal chords and wear down your voice before you've even finished the story. Be careful out there on stage and keep a bottle of water nearby.

Another pitfall in "doing voices" is attempting to perform accents that are not your own. I don't recommend you do it. Even with the very best of intentions, it is way too easy to slide down into the realm of stereotype and offense, and that invalidates the story's point. You can say that a story takes place in Tennessee, or China, or wherever, but keep your own accent. Your vivid descriptions and vocal pacing are more than enough to carry the tale.

When it's time to tell your story, get up and move! Be animated and make eye contact. Take advantage of whatever performance space you are given by occupying the entire area, moving around and making a connection with each child and adult present. Since you do not have to read your story, there is no text to make you sit still! Look them in the eyes! Watch your audience watching you as the visual feedback will give you clues as to how well you are communicating with your group. You will notice that some members of the crowd are more absorbed in your tale than others and it will be a temptation to play more heavily toward those people. Resist that urge! Acknowledge these excited children, but work to get the rest of the group further enmeshed in your performance as well.

As a performer, do not feel self-conscious. Don't be afraid to be silly as kids love it! Of course, you don't want them to be embarrassed on your behalf, but generally speaking, that only happens when the kids are older. Or the children are your own.

After each performance, do a little self-assessment. Think about what you feel went really well in your performance, and what you think you may be able to improve upon. Put these things down in writing, so that you can remember them and refer back to them later. Take note not just of your own performance, but also of the environmental conditions that affected the experience for you and everyone present. How might you be able to deal with these conditions in the future? At the least, you'll be better prepared by knowing about things that may happen. Also, seek feedback from your clients.

Try to get an audience as you practice and develop your storytelling. Perhaps you know someone (or could introduce yourself to someone) at a school, library, or day care center who could let you come in every so often to share a story or two. Try to present yourself to different groups of children and adults rather than the same one or two groups time after time. Every group is different. Storytelling is a living and breathing art. Your audiences and their differences are a large part of that living and breathing. If you think every group is going to sit back and just soak in what you say, and all react the exact way you'd imagined, you will be very wrong! You need to practice because you need to be prepared for anything. Children will often have something to say. They'll tell you they've "seen this movie." They'll just start to repeat words they think are funny. Every time I tell a story, even after years in the business, it's a different experience. But don't be scared; just be prepared. Know your story, but be prepared to be pulled off course by the audience or situation. Be prepared to choose to go in a different direction. You are not a movie.

Take time to watch other storytellers. When you have the opportunity to see other storytellers at work, do so. Watch, listen, and enjoy. Don't beat yourself up because you don't think you can ever be as good. Don't judge them because you don't think they fit your definition of storyteller or are not as good as you. Don't copy other storytellers. Do observe what speaks to you about their style and consider experimenting with how that thing about their performance might be adaptable to your own style. Or simply just sit back and enjoy! We are not all supposed to be the same. Develop and present that which is special about you.

What about props? One thing I love about storytelling is that this is an art that connects people imagination-to-imagination. You do not need a crown to tell a story about a king, you do not need wings to tell a story about a fairy, and you do not need live creatures to tell stories about animals.

Now, there are professional storytellers who are famous for using props to great effect: some tell with puppets, others with magic, and still others by drawing as they tell. Just make sure that any prop or twist you incorporate suits you well, and doesn't end up becoming a burden to you and your performance. Consider starting small, seeing how it works, and then deciding upon whether to keep the addition as-is, change it a bit, slowly expand it, or drop it altogether. You can always pick it back up and try it again later.

What to wear? Make your apparel suit your purpose. If you are a teller of historical tales, for instance, you may or may not wish to wear clothing that represents the era of your stories. For while it's interesting to tie your look into your act, and while you want to be memorable, you don't want your audience to be distracted from the story you are telling. Similarly, you do not want to distract yourself with your costuming with, for example, hats that squeeze too tight or fall over your eyes, or by hems that cause you to trip. I suggest you try comfortable, functional clothing that may in some way suggest your theme, but also gives off a "normal" look that the children will be ready to settle down and get lost in the world of your story. As with everything else, you can experiment, start out small and try new things from time to time as you feel more comfortable.

Working with Clients

Your relationship with your clients is important. Communication and reliability are key to success! When you have a gig, keep in contact with your client, even calling or e-mailing a day or two before your session to confirm and reassure them you will indeed be there. Be punctual. Arrive early, not just on time. This shows that you are friendly, adaptable, and happy to be there. At the end of the program, don't forget to thank your hosts! Thank them before you leave the location.

Within a few days after your performance, send them an e-mail with a written thank-you and a polite request for feedback. You'll leave a good and lasting final impression and you could end up with a few words to help you develop your performance and maybe have new testimonials for your publicity material!

Let me say something about publicity material and getting to be better known as a storyteller. Being a storyteller is one thing, while marketing yourself as one is another thing entirely. For the purposes of this essay, let me just share the simplest (and cheapest) of very first steps. Do you remember those previously mentioned teachers and librarians who are letting you get some experience with their groups? Ask them to spread the word among their colleagues and contacts! And ask them to write recommendations for you to be used in your publicity materials. A web presence is a must, and there are good free options, such as blogging sites and social-media sites which will allow you to talk about your services, publicize your upcoming storytelling appearances, and share photographs. If you are already using one of those services on a personal basis, create a separate "storyteller" page to keep your material focused and your services easy to find.

Good luck in pursuing your storytelling dreams. Your career may develop slowly, but I hope you enjoy your story as it unfolds. Keep researching, practicing, and evaluating, and you'll enjoy seeing your own style evolving and you'll enjoy making all of those kids and families smile! Put all of that practice to work, and show what you love about your stories. Remember: be ready for anything. Be excited about storytelling for children. Let it show in your face and in your energy as you perform.

About the Author:

 Storyteller John Weaver is a parent, performer and Early Childhood Educator based in the San Francisco Bay Area. Through his energetic, interactive, humor-filled performances, John aims to capture the attention and imagination of all ages, to educate, and to encourage children and families to continue the adventure at home by reading together.

Visit Storyteller John Weaver online at his website at:
http://www.storytellerjohnweaver.com.

How to be a Storyteller For Family Audiences

Author: Glenda Bonin

Over the years I have enjoyed telling stories to just about every group imaginable, and I love it when I'm asked to be a storyteller for a family audience. It is fun to plan for the delightful mix of ages, interests and expectations to be found in a family group. I enjoy the challenge of telling stories to families, because it means I must "stay on my toes" to keep this often-unpredictable group happy. Being a storyteller for a family audience can be a rewarding and satisfying experience, as long as you stay alert, are flexible and maintain a sense of humor.

In this chapter, I share some of the things I have learned about family audiences, so you will be ready to jump right in and enjoy every family storytelling gig you get to do. I hope what I have learned will help you develop a happy and enthusiastic following of people asking you to tell your stories again and again.

Common Traits of Family Audiences

Before I discuss some of the family audiences you might encounter, I'd like to tell you what most of them have in common.

• A family audience usually means there will be children present, from babies in arms to reluctant teens who might want to be doing something else. When children are present, parents are happy to relax a bit and give the storyteller the responsibility of keeping the kids occupied for a while.

•Unless you are told otherwise, a family audience appreciates stories with good messages, positive characters and satisfying endings.

• A family audience is usually not interested in sitting still for a full hour of storytelling, so be sure to plan for a variety of stories and be ready to identify where you can step up the pace of your program by actively engaging the group.

• Because of the possibility of wide differences in the ages present in a family audience, a storyteller should be prepared to adjust a story line-up during the performance.

Types of Family Audiences

Family audiences come together for a variety of reasons, and the foundation for each group is determined by the purpose of the event, where it is held and who has organized it. Here are a few examples of different family audiences, what you might expect and what to plan for if you accept a booking for these groups:

1. A local library where family programs are often provided as an extra event to complement the story-time schedule.

In this family program, you can expect to find more small children than adults in the audience. Short stories and participation are essential here. I usually approach these shows with the idea to please the predominant age group I see before me as the session begins. To get ready for this, I prepare different story line ups, one for each of the following groups: Pre-K (ages 3-5), K-2 (ages 5-8) and 3-4 (ages 8-10). When a storyteller keeps the kids happy at the library, this usually means that the adults are happy, too. Do not be surprised if a curious child comes in a bit too close, talks back during a story at unusual times or announces that they have to go to the bathroom. This is all part of this venue, so take this in with lots of smiles and acceptance. Your task for this venue is to keep the kids engaged. The parents love it when you don't let little interruptions get to you while you handle yourself with aplomb. This kind of family storytelling can really be fun.

2. A birthday party at the home of a youngster in the family.

Storytelling for a birthday party in someone's home is usually for kids between the ages of 4 and 10. I have found that the storytelling part for these celebrations is usually best scheduled a half-hour after the announced start of the party, and just before the cake and ice cream is served. As a rule, the parents join the session on the sidelines. At these family events, the focus is on the birthday celebration, and I have found that including the birthday child in a story is a very good idea. I am always delighted when parents approach me after the stories to talk about how wonderful it is to see children listening so intently. Many often tell me they intend to add more stories and books to their interaction with their children in the future.

3. A gathering in the park or other outside area to celebrate a family anniversary or special event.

This is one of the most difficult family storytelling events you will face since there are so many variables to consider. Outside storytelling usually means dealing with weather conditions, airplanes overhead, cars passing by, train whistles, music in the background and other people milling around in the area. I am sure you get the idea. Yet many families plan such events and ask storytellers to entertain. What should you do? To begin with, understand that you might not be up to the stress of an outside event. It is good to know your limits. For a storyteller to do a good job, it helps to have the hide of a rhinoceros, but it can be done. It is also helpful if you have your own battery-powered sound system. You will need it. Also, these gigs seldom start on time, so plan your day accordingly.

4. A family-literacy night at a school.

Family literacy celebrations at schools are heaven-sent for storytellers. Families are there to have a good time, learn about authors, buy books and listen to stories. What could be better? The problem is that these events can be a bit chaotic, but as a rule storytelling is the perfect addition for families to enjoy together. If you book such a show, be sure to ask for the storytelling area to be located in a quiet space with comfortable seating. Also, be certain that the organizers promote the story session with the start time and clear directions about where to find it.

5. A family reunion held in a rented venue such as a guest ranch or hotel.

If you'd like an exciting and challenging storytelling venue, the family reunion is for you. These gatherings fall into two camps: young families with lots of kids, and families where three (or more) generations are present. Once you succeed as a storyteller for either one of these groups, you can be confident that you are ready for almost any gig out there.

One thing to keep in mind about a family reunion is that the celebration will probably not go as planned. There's a good chance some unanticipated surprises will happen - from misunderstood communication with the rented venue and/or from family members who have not seen each other for a long time. A family reunion is sort of like a wedding when it comes to potential problems and emotional tension. All this might intrude on the great show you have planned, so come ready to be as calm and adaptable as possible. Trust me, your presenter will thank you and may even add a tip to your fee.

When you book a reunion for young families, be sure to ask for a count on the number of kids who will be present and determine the average age or grade level of children expected. You need to know how many babies, toddlers, students in grades K-2, 3-5, 6-8, teens, and young adults will be there. Your stories must satisfy the largest age-range group present. As it is with other family storytelling events, it is your job to make the children as happy as possible, so keep the show upbeat, inclusive and age-appropriate. Be prepared with several different story lineups in case the demographics change from the time you accept the booking to when the event takes place. If your presenter wants you to tell stories after dinner or late at night, beware! Unless everyone has taken a long nap in the afternoon, your audience won't have a good time, and neither will you. The best time to tell stories to young families is mid-morning or early afternoon, after the kids have had some time to run around a bit.

For a family gathering where several generations are present, I recommend taking another approach. These events usually center on the elders in the family and recognize an anniversary or birthday. There will probably be children present, and they will need to be acknowledged during the story time, but this celebration calls for carefully selected personal stories that touch the heart and contain some humor. Historic stories about family life are also excellent for this group. I usually come prepared with a box of small household items from the early 1900s. Many of these items are interesting to every generation, and act as a springboard for family members to share stories about how things "used to be." If the opportunity arises, encourage the audience to record their stories and make a simple book of these memories. A little book like this will become a family treasure, and may be the start of a wonderful tradition for future gatherings.

Family-Storytelling Checklist

To be a storyteller for a family audience, always try to get as many details as possible about the event so you can plan appropriately. Aside from the usual venue information a storyteller needs when accepting any booking such as knowing the date, time, location and need for a sound system, you might find the following list of questions helpful as you prepare to tell stories to family groups.

• How many people are expected?

• How many adults and how many children will be there?

• What ages will be represented in this mix?

• Why is this family group coming together?

• In what sort of facility/area will the event be held?

• Where will the storytelling part of the program take place?

• Will other things be going on when the stories are told?

• How much time has been set aside for storytelling?

• Do you have a specific type of story in mind?

• What are your expectations for my portion of the event?

• Do you have any special requests?

Just looking at this list should give you a hint about the vast differences hidden in a simple request to tell stories to a family audience. Furthermore, the stories you select will vary greatly once you determine what those differences are. Another benefit of asking questions like these is the opportunity for you to determine if this particular booking is a good fit for you. It is never a good idea to accept a job if you are not certain you can deliver what the caller has in mind.

As you think about telling stories to family audiences, look at the list of stories you already have, and imagine how they might work if you are asked to entertain for a specific group. My guess is that you will start to see each story in a completely new light. In some cases, you may discover that by making a few small changes to a favorite Aesop tale, you will have a perfect story to share with the group you are considering.

Remember, there no such thing as being complacent when you book a family storytelling gig. Because of that, I have found it is not worth the effort to try to pre-package a sure-fire family story routine that will keep every group happy. The fact is that I am energized by the need to create a brand new line-up for each family audience I encounter, and I believe you will find this to be true as well. Just stay alert, be flexible, keep your sense of humor, and above all, have fun!

About the Author:

Glenda Bonin has been a performer for more than thirty years, and has made her living as a storyteller since 1996. She often tours during the summer months to deliver storytelling shows in libraries and community centers across the country. She is a resident artist in schools, a busy workshop presenter, and a teller of tales at conferences, festivals and special events. Her busy schedule includes performances for adults and seniors, children and families, and people with special needs. Glenda has five different CDs to her credit.

Find her website at:
http://www.storyworksgroup.com.

How to be a Storyteller In the Classroom

Authors: Jen and Nat Whitman

Storytelling is one of the oldest teaching techniques. For ages, story has been used to teach children the values their culture holds dear and to pass on the history of their people. The story form connects with our human brains and allows us to learn new content in an enjoyable manner. Today, we can harness this power of story in our classrooms. Stories can help us reach students with concepts central to our curriculum, while allowing children to joyously play with language, music, and movement. Don't let your students miss out on the delight of sharing a good story. Once you experience the rapt engagement that a story draws from your students, you will want to use stories every day.

But how do you become a storyteller in the classroom? Here are some steps to get started:

1. Listen to a variety of good tellers. Online sites such as Youtube.com will let you take a sneak peek at accomplished storytellers. Search for clips by Bobby Norfolk, Michael McCarty, Jay O'Callahan, Diane Ferlatte, Joe Hayes and other well-known tellers. Watching them in action will give you clues for ways you can interpret and share your own stories. There are as many ways of telling a story as there are tellers so don't try to imitate anyone. Just find your own way of storytelling. Your style might be quiet and nearly motionless. You might use a wild style with lots of actions. It doesn't matter at all. What matters is that you

make each story your own and enjoy sharing it with others.

2. Look through folktale collections to find a story you really want to share with your students. Ask your school and public librarians for their favorite books on story. They can direct you to some easy-to-learn and sure-fire tales. If you teach younger students, look for stories with opportunities for audience participation where students can join in and play with the story. Most importantly, find a story that speaks to you, that is, a story that resonates with your ideas and goals. You will spend some time with this story and hopefully will enjoy telling this tale for a lifetime, so make sure it is a story that you connect with on some level.

3. Take a moment to think about this story through the lens of your curriculum. How would you envision using this story with your students? What part of your program will it enhance? Make a list of possible connections and make a plan for when you will introduce the story to your students. We want you to know this: Storytelling is such a wonderful literacy event and community building experience. It can always be used for just those purposes. Don't feel that you have to link every story you tell to a particular benchmark. Sometimes you will share a story because it is fun or because it's a story you feel your students need to hear.

4. Follow the advice in other chapters of this book about how to learn a story. Then, practice your telling until you feel comfortable.

5. Go over the story the night before you want to use it in your class. Tell it aloud while walking around, gesturing, and using your "projecting" voice. And while you do this, visualize your students listening in front of you.

30

6. Gather your students in a setting conducive to story listening. Ideally, students will be gathered in a group in front of you. A designated storytime rug is perfect for this. If your students are seated at desks, make sure the desktops are cleared. If portable computers are in front of them be sure the lids are down. You want all eyes on you. Check for possible distractions behind your back or to the side. Never tell with someone behind you, or with students making eye contact with each other, rather than with you.

7. Just relax and let the story come out. Look around at your students as you tell. Be sure all are listening and enjoying. Storytelling is an inclusive act. Try to make eye contact with each student at some point. You are sharing your story with each of them. The well-done story event feels very personal. Be aware of this and offer it as a gift to each student.

8. Follow the story with activities that connect the tale with your curriculum needs. You can use storytelling to link with your curriculum in myriad ways. Stories offer a perfect avenue for addressing literacy standards such as Imagery, Retelling, Comprehension, Word Choice, and Making Connections. You can also use stories to help you explore concepts in other content areas such as science, math, and social studies. Use the story to identify vocabulary, to talk about story structure or to introduce new material. You can develop art or music connections to continue playing with the story. Help students learn to tell the story themselves or let them make puppets or masks and dramatize the story. There are so many ways you can let individual stories provide learning opportunities for your students throughout the year.

9. Find more tales you love. Make a list of stories you want to learn to tell.

10. Pick a new story and do it all over again! Don't forget to keep telling the stories you have already learned. Students love to revisit stories they have learned earlier in the year and your colleagues would love to have you come and share the stories you know with their classes, too. The more you tell these stories, the more they become a part of you.

11. Now that you are on your way, you might want to look at a few books with advice by other teachers who are storytellers. We advise against reading too much advice before you start your first few tellings. Just TELL and worry about technique later. When you are ready to take storytelling further, look for books by these storytellers who have written specifically about using story in the classroom: Martha Hamilton, Mitch Weiss, Bob Barton, Marni Gillard, Kendal Haven, Sherry Norfolk, Margaret Read MacDonald, Robert Rubenstein, Lynn Rubright, Jane Stetson as well as the authors of this chapter.

Perhaps this is the most important step in this process: keep on telling stories! Once you have experienced the joy of telling stories with your students and have witnessed the remarkable power story has to teach, you will not ever want to stop storytelling.

About the Authors:

Jen and Nat Whitman are storytellers and international educators who have been performing as a tandem-storytelling team for over fifteen years. Jen and Nat specialize in sharing audience-participation folktales with their family audiences. They weave rhythm, music and motion into their performances and encourage listeners to jump up and join in the fun! Originally from the United States, Jen and Nat have taught in schools in Hong Kong, Germany, and Thailand. They are currently co-authoring a new book with Margaret Read MacDonald called, "Teaching With Story."

Find their website at:
http://jenandnat.com

"Every great dream begins with a dreamer."
-Harriet Tubman

How to be a Storyteller Telling Historical Stories

Author: Karol V. Brown

Historical-portrayal storytelling can be challenging in that you are talking about someone else who actually was alive. This type of storytelling carries a lot of responsibility. You have to remember the facts and be able to make the stories interesting. These presentations can be longer than most children have experienced with storytellers.

I portray a 92-year-old version of Harriet Tubman, the most renowned conductor on the Underground Railroad. In the schools, she is a very popular historical figure that every 10-12 year-old in the United States studies. Her name and place in history is not yet as well known for the youngest schoolchildren and may be just a memory for the teenage students.

To give you some background, the Underground Railroad was a network of people, mostly freed black people but also people of every race, which provided assistance to people fleeing slavery. Because helping slaves escape was an illegal act, they used coded language to communicate much like a language used by people traveling on a train. Harriet Tubman and others like her, who went back to the South to bring people up North on the Underground Railroad, were called "conductors." The people who helped were "station masters" and their homes were called "stations" or a "safe place."

If the school has grades K-8th (usually ages 5-13) and brings all the students to the storytelling event, there are too many age groups together. Generally, I suggest splitting this group into grades K-5 for one group and then have the upper grades in a second session.

There are many challenges in historical telling such as holding the students' attention, giving information on a level of understanding for the different age groups, and staying in character when answering the students' questions. Those question-and-answer sessions can go in any direction you can think of or even in some you have not thought of. However, with good preparation, working with all the students together can be effective and fun.

Some strategies I have found that work are:

1. Give good context clues.

For example, Harriet Tubman was a black woman who was born a slave around 1820-1821. She grew up in Maryland. Her manner of speech is different than that of the children who are listening to the stories. Her use of the words "ain't" and "folks," drawn from Southern dialect from the 1800's, may be strange to students in areas far away from states in the South. By using a mixture of a few words of the character's time and culture with the more contemporary or standard words that the students are more familiar with, you will help with the students' level of understanding.

2. Keep the audience involved.

I start out my presentation by talking to the students as Harriet Tubman from when I first I enter the room. The students are thrilled to find out that this is not just a play or performance that they can only watch. She is talking to them and asking the audience questions such as, "What is the name of your school?" "How old are you?" "I used to love to watch the eagles fly. Do you have bald eagles where you live?" Each question Harriet asks brings their attention back from where it may have drifted.

3. Keep the stories short.

Although a full program may be 45 minutes, each story in the program is only about five minutes long. These breaks from one story to the next help the students' comprehension. Even the youngest students are able to follow along with you for five minutes.

4. Use frequent transitions.

Between the stories, I use a new direction, a question, or a song. Giving the students a chance to release their pent-up energy with a sing-along moment is a great transition. This can be added when the children are starting to fidget. The older students are usually in the back of the room and more inhibited, yet still competitive when it comes to the younger students. You can challenge them to participate by saying, "I am sure this side of the room is the loudest group, what do you think?" This encourages the students to sing just a little louder than if they had not been put on the spot.

5. Observe and respond to the children's need to move.

With the sing-along, they can clap their hands or stand up and sing. Stories that actually give them a chance to move are great for keeping the students awake and involved. There is a need to be cautious with participatory activities. If they go on for too long a period, it will be hard to settle them back down.

6. Add humor.

Everyone loves to laugh. With historical storytelling such as with Harriet Tubman, not all the stories are happy. There are some sad parts about her life and it can really draw on the emotions of the audience. After these stories, the proper transition is a little humor. This does not mean telling a joke, but rather doing something unexpected such as a gesture, facial expression, or a humorous observation from the teller. These things can provide just the right amount of comic relief.

7. Use eye contact.

This should be a main concern for any storyteller. Every person in the room should feel like you have looked right at them. Scan the audience, front, back and on all sides. Don't move fast like a water sprinkler, but take the time to look at someone for a few seconds, then someone behind or in front of them. Switch to the other side of the room and work down the aisles with your eyes. When the children's hands go up to answer your questions, keep good eye contact and call out the color of their clothes to identify who you are calling on to ask their question. When children are involved in your stories, they love that you know they are there with you.

When I am Harriet Tubman, I am teaching children that history is real. Right in front of their eyes, what they've read in a book is being reenacted. Their little minds are busy developing questions. You never know what thoughts are developing while you tell the stories. One of my favorite questions was from a little boy in elementary school, hearing how Harriet had come to a river one night on a trip back up North and, not finding a bridge or a boat to cross it, had to wade through the icy-cold water. His question was, "Why didn't you use some wood to make a boat?" There are some questions you just can't find answers to in a book. Some questions are challenging, and that makes it fun to come up with an answer.

Historical storytelling is rewarding in many ways. To have children sit still and listen is by itself something that teachers find remarkable. But when you realize that they are listening and it is creating some constructive thinking, it means you have added some fuel to their desire to learn.

About the Author:

Karol Brown is a registered dietitian and health educator with natural talent for public speaking and teaching. She lives in Washington State with her husband James.

For over 12 years, Karol and James, as "Brown Tones Productions," have presented a historical portrayal of Harriet Tubman. Karol is "Aunt Harriet" to the many people she has touched in her presentation of Harriet as a charming, jovial and inspirational elderly woman. Using humor, drama, and audience interactions, Karol, a consummate storyteller, brings to life the stories of the woman called Moses.

After sixteen years of research on Harriet Tubman and twelve years of telling her stories, Karol combined research and storytelling into a book, "30 Lessons in Love, Leadership and Legacy from Harriet Tubman." This book is being used to teach leadership to youth in schools, churches and community centers.

Find her website at:
http://www.visitharriettubman.com.

How to be a Storyteller Around a Campfire

Author: Tim Ereneta

There is something about sitting around a campfire and staring into the flames that invites a story. I have been fortunate to step into the role of the storyteller on many occasions around a fire, sometimes as a camp counselor, sometimes as a parent, and sometimes as an invited performer.

Campfire storytelling sessions are varied. They range from a casual gathering of friends or family members around a fire pit in a campground or backyard, to a more formal interpretive session for dozens of park visitors in an outdoor amphitheater, to being part of a lively night of songs, skits, and entertainment at a gathering of Scouts or children attending summer camp.

For me, telling stories around a fire can be one of the most enjoyable environments for storytelling, but I have also learned there are plenty of complications when it comes to performing near a fire, complications that don't typically arise when telling in a corporate setting or a school classroom. For example, the primary concern for a campfire session is safety, both for the storyteller and the audience. Fire, even when contained in a fire pit or fireplace, can be unpredictable, and you want your audience to remember your stories, not an accident or injury.

Keep Safety First

1. Make sure that your venue has fire suppression materials nearby.

Depending on the space, this could be a bucket of water, a hose, sand, or a fire extinguisher. Designate a responsible person to be in charge of fire safety, a "fire marshal," who is keeping an eye on loose sparks and embers, and will move to extinguish any accidental fires.

2. Take charge of audience seating.

Before the program, adjust the audience seating (whether this is log benches or camping chairs), if this is possible. Create a zone around the entire fire pit that is free of chairs or obstacles. Only you and your fire marshal will enter this zone. Make sure that your listeners will be seated where they can see the fire and feel its warmth, but they are far enough away to avoid any sparks or embers that the fire may emit.

3. Try to avoid the smoke.

Campfires will give off smoke; it's an inevitable by-product of combustion. Start the fire well before the storytelling begins, so that as your audience arrives, they can see which way the wind is blowing the smoke and where smoke is less likely to be an irritation. Winds do shift, however, and smoke can eddy, so be prepared (especially in smaller environments, such as a family campsite) for listeners to move themselves and their seats while listening to your stories.

You may want to tell your stories from a standing position, so that you can move easily if the wind shifts the smoke into your eyes, nose, and throat. This is why you've already set up a zone around the fire that has no obstacles, so you can move freely to a smoke-free area.

4. Tell the audience about safety.

Guidelines for safety should be made clear to all attendees at the beginning of the program. Remind children to refrain from throwing pinecones, sticks, and rocks into the fire. Here's an important tip: ask your designated fire marshal to make these announcements.

Dealing with Distractions

Another concern for outdoor fireside-storytelling sessions are the many possibilities for distractions. To minimize these, follow these guidelines:

1. Be aware of the fire.

You will be focusing on your audience, and on your story, but if your fire erupts with a sudden dramatic surge of flame as a new log catches, or if the fire snaps and sends a shower of sparks out of the fire pit, you should pause in your telling. At that moment, your audience's respective brains, hard-wired for survival, will direct their attention to what the fire is doing. By acknowledging the fire, even silently, you are reassuring your listeners that you are taking care of them.

Although the shape and size of a fire will change over time, ask your helper to add logs or stoke the fire in between stories, rather than in the midst of one, or arrange a nonverbal signal between the two of you to pause the story if tending the fire is needed.

2. Keep flashlights off.

Ask your audience to keep flashlights off during the program. As it gets dark, a beam of light from a flashlight not only will distract other audience members, but if it shines in your eyes, it can temporarily blind you. (Your pupils have been looking out in the dark at your audience, rather than at the brightness of the fire).

3. Save the S'mores for later.

If a program includes roasting marshmallows, do this before or after (not during) the storytelling, especially if children or families are in attendance. Young children often need assistance with this time-honored campfire tradition, and can be quite vocal with their excitement if their marshmallow catches fire or falls off into the fire, as well as with their frustration at the time it takes to roast the perfect golden brown marshmallow. If it is part of the program, make it clear to the audience when this activity will take place (e.g., "we are going to hear two stories, and then we will roast marshmallows, starting with Cabin 3"). If there are lots of children who will be engaged in this activity, you should designate several adult helpers to supervise.

4. Check to be sure you can be heard.

Most campfire programs are outside. If you are at an amphitheater that has an amplified sound system, use it. In most outdoor settings, you will not have access to such equipment, so you need to prepare your voice to be heard. I think every storyteller should have a good 15 to 25 minute vocal warmup. Being too quiet prevents listeners from entering into the storytelling event, and is more likely to distract others.

Content for Campfire Storytelling

Considering the logistics of the campfire storytelling event is just one aspect of preparing for the session. As you get ready to tell stories, the question of content arises. What kind of stories should you tell at a campfire?

Any type of story can be suited for an outdoor session around a fire. If you're part of an interpretive program at a park or historic site, your theme is likely already determined. You may have stories or legends about the site, or traditional tales that help explain the behavior of native animals or the creation of various landforms. If the theme of the program is open, however, one question typically arises, especially from the audience: "Are you going to tell scary stories?"

I've heard this question asked by young children, sometimes with anxiety, sometimes with excitement, and by parents or older adults recalling (with delight or dismay) being scared out of their wits as a child at a campfire ghost story.

The question of whether or not to tell scary stories at a campfire is a decision you will need to make. Personally, if I have a choice in selecting material, I do not tell frightening stories in the dark to children or family audiences. Partly this is due to my background as a camp counselor: with children sleeping away from home for the first time in a strange environment, complete with strange noises and an unfamiliar landscape, my colleagues and I did not want to increase the children's anxiety levels, especially right before bedtime. In addition, as part of my promotion of storytelling as an art form, I want to give a positive impression to listeners of all ages and not terrify them. Given a receptive audience

45

for stories at campfire programs, I am happy to share a variety of styles of story. For me, folk tales and wonder tales go over well with young audiences. With older crowds, depending on the mood, ancient myths and wisdom tales seem an apt fit for the reflective environment brought on by the embers of a fire.

Like many storytellers, however, during the weeks leading up to Halloween, I have been asked to prepare a program of scary stories to tell around the campfire. But I will discuss with the client in advance what the age of the audience will be. For an audience that includes children under the age of eight, my stories may be full of ghosts, witches, and vampires, but none of the stories are intended to be frightening. These "spooky" stories are full of Halloween images, but I am careful to select stories that have happy or silly endings. I find that children between the ages of 8 and 12 appreciate jump tales, where a spooky story ends with a loud "Boo!" or other surprising sound. Engaging the startle reflex of the audience allows them to be scared for just a moment. For this age group, I tend to rely on world folk tales with macabre imagery in the form of supernatural creatures (demons in the shapes of rats, talking skeletons) but there's always a happy ending: the hero outwits the monsters. It is only for high school audiences and adults that I tell the bloody ghost stories, with family members buried alive, corpses returning from the dead to seek revenge, or when creepy things that go bump in the night triumph.

However, I want to reiterate that any type of story can work in a campfire setting. Whatever genre of stories you end up telling, whether they be tall tales, ghost stories, sacred stories, fables, or true-life stories, you will be participating in a tradition dating back to earliest human history: gathering together in the dark, around a source of warmth and light, to exercise our imaginations.

About the Author:

Tim Ereneta is a storyteller based in the city of Berkeley, California, specializing in telling fairy tales to adult audiences. He has told stories at festivals, on stages, and in house concerts, and learned to tell stories around a campfire as a summer camp counselor in California. Tim also writes about storytelling at his blog, "Breaking the Eggs: Performance Storytelling in the 21st Century," at: http://storytelling.blogspot.com.

Find his website at:
http://www.timereneta.com.

**All storytelling experiences need
an audience, a story, and a storyteller**.

How to be a Storyteller In a Library Setting

Author: Elly Reidy

Commitment to the development of life-long readers is a goal of most librarians. This begins in early-literacy programs, such as story times, designed for various age groups from babies through pre-school, and continues in programming aimed at school-aged children through teens. Storytelling for these audiences can be challenging, but for the early-literacy crowd there are several ways to include storytelling in the story-time setting.

Baby Time

A Baby-Time program is generally focused on infants through 18-month-old toddlers. Besides being an introduction to books, finger plays, songs, and movement, these youngest library patrons are being exposed to the sounds and rhythms of language.

Repetition and movement are key for this age child. Even an infant will watch the movement in the room, and will hear the cadence of the repeated sounds. The story doesn't need to be very short either if there is constant movement. Having the adults in the room, in full participation, saying the words in unison and doing the motions with these little ones reinforces both the sound and movement of language. A great story for this age group is "The Bear Hunt."

Before the program begins, "hide" a large bear puppet within your reach, along with several other animal puppets, perhaps chosen to coordinate with that week's story theme. Begin with the refrain.

The refrain is:

"We're goin' on a bear hunt." (Slap legs as if walking.)
"We're goin' on a bear hunt." (Slap legs as if walking.)
"I'm not afraid!" (Hands in fists, bend arms up at the elbow, shake arms back and forth in time to the words.)
"I'm not afraid!" (Hands in fists, bend arms up at the elbow, shake arms back and forth in time to the words.)

"Open the door." (Open the door while making a squeaking sound.)
"Close the door. SLAM!" (Close the door. Clap hands together on "SLAM!")
"And down the path." (Resume slapping legs as if walking.)
Repeat refrain.

"Open the gate." (Open the gate while making a squeaky sound.)
"Close the gate." (Close the gate while making a squeaky sound.)
"And through the grass." (Rub hands together, make swishing sound.)
Repeat refrain.

"Oh look! Here's a lake." (Hands on face near mouth as if startled.)
"Dive in and swim, swim, swim, swim, swim, swim, swim, swim, swim, swim, swim, swim, swim!" (Dive and swim.)
"Shake off all that water!" (Shake your body.)
Repeat refrain.

"Oh look! Here's a swamp!" (Hands on face near mouth as if startled.)

"Eeewww! Squish, squish, squish, squish, squish, squish, squish, squish, squish, squish, squish, squish, squish!" (Move feet on the floor as if walking through the swamp.)

"Shake off all that mud!" (Stamp feet.)

Repeat refrain.

"Oh look! Here's a river!" (Hands on face near mouth as if startled.)

"Let's untie our boat and get in." (Untie the boat and get in. Sing "Row, Row, Row Your Boat" two times while making the rowing motion.)

"OK, now tie up our boat!" (Tie up the boat.)

Repeat refrain, but whisper because you have arrived at the bear's cave.

"Let's see if we can find the bear."

Pull out the "wrong" puppets, one at a time, and say, "This is not a bear! What is this?" After each one is identified, ask what sound that animal makes. Have the parents and young children call for the bear and finally bring it out of hiding. Have the bear whisper in your ear that it wants to give hugs but that it wants to go back to the library to do that. Reverse your "journey" but travel very fast doing the appropriate motions.

"Let's run down the path, get in our boat, untie it, (sing "Row Your Boat" twice, really fast), tie up our boat, run through the swamp, swim through the lake, run through the grass, open the gate, close the gate, up the path, open the door, close the door!"

Repeat refrain, but say,

"We went on a bear hunt!"

Toddler Time

Most toddler programs are designed for children 18-36 months. This age group tends to be mobile in the story-time room so interactive is the way to go. Control of the energy in a room full of toddlers and their caregivers is much, much easier if you are free to concentrate on a story rather than a book. Try using a puppet or a story prop such as a topsy-turvy doll, or flannel figures to tell a simple story. The key for this age group is to keep it short and simple. The key for the storyteller is to practice, practice, practice!

To ease into this, try using a short, well-illustrated picture book you know well enough that you don't need to read it. Hold the book in front of you and turn the pages as you tell the story. Make eye contact with the toddlers by letting your gaze travel the room. Watch their reactions and their responses to the cadence of your voice as you adjust the volume and the speed of the story. Don't rush, but don't dawdle. The toddlers will watch the pictures and watch you as they listen. This could be the first time they have been told a story, and you were the one to do it!

Once you can move away from holding the book, try using a hand puppet with a moveable mouth as narrator. Again, use a story you know well and have the puppet help you tell the story. Practice using a different voice for the puppet so it is clear who is speaking. To the toddler, the puppet is real so respond to the puppet naturally and conversationally. When the story is over and you take the puppet off of your hand, lay the puppet down gently as you would a sleeping child. Tossing this "person" aside sends the wrong message.

The puppet you use for telling stories is a tool, not a toy. The toddlers will want to play with the puppet but this cannot happen! This puppet has to stay with you as part of the "magic" of the storytelling experience. Make the puppet unavailable by putting it out of sight.

The same goes for flannel figures or story props. These are tools of the trade, not toys. Like most library workers, you have put a lot of time and money into building the story kit and as each item is needed, you will need to protect your investment.

Preschoolers

This age group, generally three-to-six year olds, is able to listen to a longer story. They can comprehend more than they can articulate and you can push the envelope when both reading and telling them stories. Pay attention to the general "feel" of the crowd as they are coming to Story Time, as you may have to revamp your planned program. Usually all it takes is the routine of the opening activities to get these little ones focused and ready to listen.

Story props, puppets and flannel stories are well received. You can use the same steps to ease into the process you may have used with the toddler crowd, but know that preschoolers love stories already, and many of them are moving up from Toddler Time. They understand sequencing and they have broader vocabularies. They can focus for longer periods of time and a five-minute story, well practiced and well told, is not outside their capability. Try this technique called "storyboarding."

Choose a familiar story, perhaps a short fable or a familiar folktale, say, "The Little Red Hen." Read the story several times, out loud. Be aware of the rhythm of the story, of the repeated phrases and the different characters. Use a sheet of blank paper and draw a grid, maybe 12 to 15 squares. In sequence, draw a stick figure picture of the action of the story in the squares, making more squares if you need them.

Tell yourself the story as you look at the pictures you've drawn. Tell it again. Now turn the paper over and tell the story again. Check your pictures if you get stuck, but keep going to the end. Try it again, without looking at the pictures. If you have to look, that's okay. You're learning a new skill and you need to be as patient with yourself as you would be with someone you were training. Give yourself time to get comfortable and practice until you can tell the story without looking at the pictures.

Some people practice while looking in a mirror. Others practice telling the story to the wall or to a pet. Find what works best for you. Keep practicing the story out loud and pay attention to how you are saying what you are saying. Do you need a pause here, a little more volume there? Should you try different voices for the characters? It's YOUR story, and this is supposed to be fun, so you can be as detailed as you are comfortable being! However, don't overwhelm the simplicity of the story with accents, music, characterizations and activities. Be the vessel the story comes in, be its voice.

Because a library worker's goal is to promote reading, consider having copies of the actual book on display. Introduce the story by announcing to your audience you are going to tell them a story rather than read it. American children are not exposed to storytelling generally, so they may ask you to show them the pictures. You could tell them to "think up their own pictures" as they listen to the story being told.

54

As you begin telling "The Little Red Hen," perhaps using different voices for the characters, encourage the children to say the repeated phrases with you. You may be surprised at how quickly preschoolers know what part they are supposed to say and when they should be listening! Never underestimate this audience. Preschoolers are far more story savvy than most adults expect and they love, love, love a good story! They are a very appreciative audience and want to be a part of the experience. The more they get to participate, the better they like it, and it's more fun for you, too.

You now have a new skill, the children have a new experience, and the parents are impressed with the high quality and variety of the story time. As a bonus for your library, your branch will have increased circulation because you, forward-thinking library worker, have provided a stack of every available picture book of the story you just told and many children will want to check one out to take home. So it's win, win, win!

School Groups

School-aged children have an even greater capacity for listening to stories and most library visits involve a story time. Mixing more complex stories, both reading and telling, makes for a very satisfying story experience!

Develop a themed set of stories or weave stories you know with some reading favorites into a 30-minute program. Use the storyboarding technique to learn a new story quickly. Read a couple, tell one, read another one, tell another one. Mix it up.

As you learn more stories and can offer longer storytelling programs, begin to market that to neighborhood schools. Storytelling meets most state standards for language arts and teachers will use the storytelling experience of the students in classroom activities. In these days of budget cuts and downsizing, this partnership can build a stronger community, improve a student's language skills and provide another resource for parents. Increased book circulation at the library is nice, too.

Final Thoughts

Materials used in story time, either read or told, fall under the "Fair Use" clause in the copyright laws. Materials used with school groups, either in the library or in the classroom, are also permissible. If you are presenting a program on your own time and are being paid, ethically and legally, you need permission from the author and, sometimes, the publisher to use another person's creative work. Materials in the public domain, such as most folklore, are freely available. There may be cultural considerations you should observe, and researching a story thoroughly will help you learn what these might be.

Consider purchasing your own copy of any story you tell since children's books go out of print very quickly. Stories tend to evolve and change with the telling, so keeping the original work as a touchstone will help keep the story true to the author's intent as you make the story your own. If there is something you think you are going to use for a few years, it's best to own it rather than to learn it has been weeded out of the collection due to low circulation or because someone has loved that book to tatters!

If you use flannel figures, a prop, or a puppet with a story, create a container large enough for all of the pieces and a copy of the book. This keeps your materials organized, easily accessible and protected from wear and tear.

Visit secondhand stores for puppet bargains, peruse the internet for story props and inexpensive books and read professional library journals for ideas, story themes and trends. Keep current, but remember that many children are no longer exposed to classic children's literature. You may think "The Three Little Pigs" is too familiar a story. It isn't, not in this age of digital everything, and besides, kids enjoy hearing the same stories over and over again. You do remember babysitting?

If you live near a college, check their course offerings for storytelling classes. Read constantly. There may be a storytelling guild in your area whose members can be a great resource for you and may provide a safe place to try out new material. Read. Look for information about storytelling festivals, story slams, (friendly storytelling competitions), and folk festivals. Read folk tale collections. Find stories you enjoy and learn to tell them well. Read.

Finally, accept that there will be days you cannot do storytelling with your groups. Kids are going to be amped up if the barometer is rising or falling, if the wind is blowing, or they have a new puppy, a new baby or Grandma is finally in town. Some days it will work and some days it won't. If it's not working, stop for the day. You haven't failed. You have successfully read your audience and are meeting the need at that time. Try again later in the session, or leave it for the next session. Over the course of time, this audience will look forward to the storytelling part of their library visit, and they will ask for their favorites, over and over and over again.

About the Author:

Elly Reidy has 27 years of experience working with children in schools, churches, civic events and libraries, and has worked as a storyteller since 1998. She is a three-time member of the Nu Wa Storytelling Delegation to China, and her on-going association with this project has given her opportunities to share stories in a Chinese village as well as the International School of Beijing, building bridges of understanding via the power of storytelling.

She has been a member of the National Storytelling Network since 2002, and graduated from the Storytelling Institute at South Mountain Community College in 2007. She has led workshops for high-school child development classes, Headstart Teacher Inservice Programs, Middle School ESL classes and student and teacher workshops at the International School of Beijing.

Find more information at:
http://www.ellyreidy.com

How to be a Storyteller With Adolescents and Teens

Author: K. Sean Buvala

Human beings are hard-wired to understand and process stories. This subconscious understanding of story does not come upon us at birth and then suddenly vanish at 10 years old, only to reappear when we have finally passed through adolescence. For the term "adolescence," I am thinking of ages 10-20, give or take a few years. These years, mostly a time of adapting to social, cultural and peer-related norms, include both puberty and the teen years. I have spent many years of my adult life working with adolescents and their families. I know this for sure: Yes, you can tell stories to, for and with adolescents. You just need to know what to expect.

1. Expect to find real people hidden within the "mysterious" adolescents.

In my years directing youth programs, I found that new volunteers believed that teenagers had some sort of extra-sensory perception (ESP) about adults. Phrases like, "They can spot a phony instantly" or "You can never fool teens, they automatically know when adults are lying" were rather common during the initial training programs. The truth is this: adolescents are no more capable of "detecting" anything about adults than adults are. Adolescents are not like dogs, who can find meaning in the slightest and most subtle movements of their masters. In fact, the relative immaturity of the early adolescents might make them less capable of "reading" adults.

What does this mean for the storyteller? It means: relax. No one in your crowd of youngsters is reading your mind or using any ESP on you. The young people before you, despite any protestations or facades they might be displaying, are, actually, just people. Some of them are mentally and emotionally mature at age 14 while some 21-year-olds still cannot figure out basic manners. You are dealing with real people in the midst, in most cases, of rapid development. Just be yourself and do not try to be what you think your audience of young people wants you to be. Mostly, they want to know that you will not be b-o-r-i-n-g.

2. Expect that you will need to challenge the storyteller stereotype.

Here is where you need to be aware of a challenge. Storytelling, at least in my part of the world, is still perceived by both adults and adolescents as something that the "little kids" get at the library or is the bedtime ritual for preschool-aged children. When you are telling for adolescents, I want you to lead off with your best "you really have no idea what I am going to tell you" type of story.

For example, I specialize in telling folk and fairytales, especially from the Grimm Brothers. Trust me, when I tell this to an audience of adolescents, their eyes begin to roll back into their heads as they proleptically pass out from the potential for boredom. So, I will lead my teen programs with a darker Grimm tale such as "Seven Ravens," where the young heroine, whose brothers have been turned into ravens, must pass bravely through the threats of being eaten by the moon and sun only to find that she must cut off her finger in order to save her feathery siblings. Told well, adolescents (both boys and girls) in the seats begin to squirm and shake their heads as the knife makes its first appearance. Because I use a lot of foreshadowing, the self-mutilation soon is enough to shake any remnants of this-is-like-story-time thinking from these young minds.

I told this story of loyalty-to-one's-family once at a festival in Canada where two very-trendy teenage women kept hiding behind their hands for fear of what might happen next in the story. It was truly a stereotype-busting moment that let my storytelling move past "this is kiddie stuff" to "let's hear what else he's got."

Once you have their attention with a strong and unusual opening, you can usually move into stories that are more complex. However, please, do not take your work or your storytelling too seriously. Keep plenty of funny stories in your program, tossing in one or more of the stories in the genre of "Seven Ravens" just to keep them on their metaphorical toes.

3. Expect the need to keep them on their real toes, too.

Depending on where you are storytelling, you may need to add some quick group-movement games to your program. This is especially true in schools and weekend-long events or conferences. In my business workshops, I would not keep adults sitting for much more than 20 minutes at a stretch without some type of break or opportunity to interact. Just like those adult learners and the library's wiggly toddlers, your adolescents cannot be expected to sit quietly while you babble on. Be audience focused in both your story choices and your group-interaction moments. Take the time to say to your adolescent audience, "Stand up and tell someone what you think the secret meaning of that last story was all about." You will want to keep your program lists filled with these types of quick-to-do movement games. Search the

Internet and your local bookstore for anthologies of short crowd games and activities.

4. Expect unusual eye contact.

As you read this book, you will repeatedly see writings about the importance of eye contact. I have written about my experiences with young people who listen "sideways" or in non-traditional ways. When working with adolescent audiences, know that your gaze may not be returned to you. This does not mean that they are not listening. Inside the mind of any adolescent at any given time is a highway full of information that is being processed, evaluated and stored. The brain of a 14-year-old, after a few years of rest starting after early childhood, is as busy again as it was back when the child was a toddler. Your story is just one piece of data racing into their brains. Teens staring right at you might not hear a word you say as they think about the hundreds of text messages they are missing while you talk. The teenager that never looks up at you, staring through the window as you speak, might be deeply engrossed in any number of levels in your story. Good storytellers, telling to this age group, keep offering eye contact, while knowing that their responsibility is the delivery of the story-message and not the assurance that the teens "get it."

5. Expect noise.

Generally, the younger the adolescents are in your group, the more they will be very vocal with you as you tell your stories. Audiences of small children can be noisy with age-appropriate but self-absorbed comments such as "me too" or "That happened to me once." Little ones tend to be focused on the here-and-now, seeing everything through the lens of concrete thinking. However, your adolescent audiences start to discover abstract thinking right around the ages of 10-11. Now, when you say, "She cut off her finger with the knife," some young person with freshly-minted thinking skills might shout out, "She's gonna bleed to death!" It is possible that the young person who shouts out will have even surprised themselves with their outburst. This is what happens when abstract thinking mixes with the non-existent self-editing skills of a child. Treat these noises and interjections just as you treat them when 5-year-olds shout out things about themselves as you are storytelling: acknowledge the concern or idea if appropriate and then move on quickly.

6. Expect deeper understanding that might surprise you.

Be ready for some surprises, too. That new abstract thinking in the kids' brains can really pay off.

Into every youth program comes that one kid who cannot hold still, who can't seem to focus and you are never sure if they hear a single thing you say. For whatever reason, Carl was always wired and moving about, like a teenage boy made entirely of springs.

One fall weekend many years ago, Carl and 25 other young men attended a conference where I was using stories and storytelling as the principle teaching method. On the first evening, I began by telling what I call the first half of the "Iron John" story from the Grimm Brothers. I take the story up to the point where the young prince jumps onto Iron John's shoulders and they head into the forest. While I had the apparent attention of most of the group, it appeared through his fidgeting and squirming that Carl's mind was everywhere but in the room with the rest of us.

After a moment to let the story sink in, I asked the group, "So what? Why would I tell you that story?"

Carl's hand shot up but his mouth was already running before I could call on him. For the next 20 minutes, about twice as long as it actually takes to tell the story, Carl talked on about every aspect of the story, both literal and metaphorical. I had to prod him a few times to help him get the order of the story correct, but he clearly had not only heard my story but in the 11 minutes of my storytelling, had gone to a much deeper place than any of the other students in the group.

What a great moment when the adolescent that isn't supposed to understand the transcendent levels of a story actually gets it. Adolescents hear your stories, they react to your stories and, sometimes, they even surprise you with their interpretations from your stories.

Throughout this "How to be a Storyteller" book, you will be able to learn more about the specifics of learning and telling stories. I hope that these six expectations make it easier for you to work specifically with the adolescents that you will encounter in your storytelling programs.

About the Author:

Sean Buvala, storytelling since 1986, is the founder and director of Storyteller.net, which commemorates 15 years of service with the release of this book. Sean has written many books and resources, including "Measures of Story: How to Create a Story from Floats and Anecdotes."

Find Sean's website at:
http://www.seantells.com.

How to be a Storyteller With Adults

Author: Chris King

Very often, when I tell someone I am a storyteller, they will say, "Oh, how nice. Do you tell stories to children in the schools and at the libraries?" They are surprised when I answer, "Yes, I do tell stories to children of all ages, but I also tell stories to adults." It is my opinion that adults want and need stories even more than the children do.

When I have been hired to do a storytelling program at an event that will attract families - for example, a county or state fair, a museum benefit, an outdoor festival, or a family celebration – I notice as I share my stories that it is the adults who are hanging on every word. They love to participate, even if just through intense listening.

Interaction and participation are important in storytelling. Everyone loves a good story. Make sure to find stories that you love and love to tell others. Practice often by asking family members and friends to listen to your stories. Before you know it, you will be able to form a bond and special rapport with audience members. Our favorite stories become their stories, and they will internalize those stories and take them away with them forever.

One of the first and foremost ways to raise the level of energy in an audience is to use humor. Laughter serves as energizing exercise. When we all laugh together, we immediately form a bond with each other. Everyone loves to laugh, so start with a funny story and give everyone time to catch up and laugh.

Subtle participation comes from taking our time to let the audience anticipate where we are going. It also comes from avoiding the use of too many descriptive details, so that our listeners can imagine and fill them in for themselves, participating with us in our stories. They picture the characters, the setting, and the scenes through their own eyes, enriching the story for them.

If you are at a reunion or family gathering, and feel comfortable asking for participation, ask family members or attendees to share a quick story. If they are uncomfortable getting up on their feet, let them tell from a chair. You will be surprised how quickly others start to volunteer to tell once they see others chiming in. When telling to a brand new audience, and those who are unfamiliar with storytelling, it may take a bit of coaxing.

Remember that we should always strive for some form of participation. The special part of being a storyteller is the personal interaction we build between audience members and ourselves. We need to give each listener the feeling that we are telling the story especially to and for him or her. One way to accomplish this is through individual eye contact. Rather than looking off or up in a different direction, try to look each person in the eye for at least three seconds before moving on to another set of eyes. They will catch your energy and you will catch theirs. This is a subtle and yet probably one of the strongest levels of participation you can achieve.

As far as using music, use call and response, finger play and even bringing people up on the stage with you to act out or take part in some other way. You must be totally comfortable with the ideas and techniques involved. That is the wonderful part of being a storyteller: there is such huge latitude of ways to tell stories. Everyone is free to be unique.

Why do we want to tell stories for adults?

Remembering and telling stories helps adults deal with life's challenges. If you have ever experienced an accident, an illness, a death, or some other horrible event, you know how much better you feel after telling about it. Often, the more times you tell it the better that you feel. And once we have shared our story or stories with other adults, they are usually reminded of a similar story that they then tell us. The beauty of the whole process is that not only do we come around to feeling better, we make new friends through the sharing. For, when you know someone's story, you can't help but like them.

During a storytelling workshop on "How to Tell Personal Stories" I told the story of my son's devastating bout with Non-Hodgkin's Lymphoma. It was at least five years later when a woman rushed up to me to tell me that my story of my son's battle had helped her so much the past year when her daughter had been diagnosed with cancer. That is the power of story.

Stories guide us through the stages and thresholds we face through life. Joseph Campbell wrote, "It has been the chief function of much of mythological lore . . .to carry . . . the individual across the critical thresholds from . . .infancy to adulthood, and from old age to death." As we listen to and tell the myths and legends of the past, we learn how to face the many stages and passages our lives take. In an abstract way, we can relate to the heroes and heroines of bygone times. Modern stories also help us with those same changes and passages.

Storytelling for adults encourages them to loosen up, remember, and then tell their stories. When I asked Donald Davis, the well-known storyteller of personal stories, what he likes most of all about being a storyteller, he told me that he just loved it when he heard people who had attended his program turning to companions and starting to tell their own stories. You will know and feel that you were successful when you see the same interactions in your audience or an audience member comes up after your storytelling session to tell you about a situation similar to one you were just telling about.

If we, as adults, consider our lives to be stories, what a delightful and creative life we will live. I believe that adults love the idea of living a life of story. Jean–Paul Sartre wrote, ". . .a man is always a teller of tales, he lives surrounded by his stories and the stories of others, he sees everything that happens to him through them; and he tries to live his life as if he were telling a story." You see, we need our stories and our family stories to give us a legacy. That legacy strengthens our tradition, our purpose, our self-worth and our reason for living the life we live. After all, I want the story I leave with my children to be a story we can all be proud of.

Here's a tip: when storytelling with adults, pick a theme for your storytelling program. Having and planning a theme for your program not only helps with the publicity and advertising, but also helps you, the storyteller, plan a cohesive performance. For example, a successful theme for mid-March is trickster tales (in preparation for April Fools' Day). Everyone and all ages enjoy them and there are plenty available. By choosing and working on these, you might gain the benefit of adding some new, fun stories to your repertoire. This will also work for other themes.

Choose a theme that revolves around a special date. This is one of the easiest ways to pick a theme. Every month has a special date or theme of its own. For February, we have Valentine's Day. This is a perfect time to tell stories that touch on love. Also in March we celebrate St. Patrick's Day. There are more Irish folktales than you can imagine. Don't try to tell with an Irish brogue, unless you have one naturally. Celebrate Earth Day by telling stories that focus on nature and animals. Another obvious theme is Halloween, probably because of the enjoyment of ghost stories. Of course, October is the most popular time for them but there is no reason to avoid ghost stories at any time of year.

Also, there are many special days and weeks throughout the year that aren't necessarily national holidays that will give you ideas for a theme. There is no reason, either, that you can't create a special day of your own to celebrate with your audience.

Pick a theme that has some special meaning for you. A newer teller I know, who is disabled, plans to work on stories that address the theme of being "different from others." There is a plethora of stories with this theme. One of my favorites is "The Ugly Duckling." What are you passionate about? If it is politics, there are many political stories. I know another teller who is fascinated by how the flowers were named, and tells stories that are all related to flowers. There are "pourquoi" ("why?" in French) stories that explain why something is the way it is. For example, the story might "explain" why a turtle's shell is cracked or why the elephant has a long nose. There are stories about justice and judges. There are stories about women, giants, mathematics and science. There is plenty of variety!

Be sure to pick a theme that interests you. I mention this warning, because as storytellers we often get calls from groups that have already picked a theme and want us to tell stories that adhere to that theme. This is fine, if it is a theme that turns you on and you feel will add an exciting dimension to your telling. But, if it doesn't interest you, don't do it. Remember the first rule of storytelling: only tell stories that you love. If you choose a theme of interest, I will guarantee that you will find stories you love that fit that theme.

So, pick a theme and get busy. Just make sure to have some fun and learn some new stories!

About the Author:

Chris King, an active member of O.O.P.S! (The Ohio Order for the Preservation of Storytelling), guest editor and presenter for the "National Storytelling Network," has been a storyteller "all of her life." Chris tells traditional tales — with a twist; original stories — personal and believable; and business stories. She also maintains a "Portfolio Career" (having a variety of careers). Chris is a writer, website designer and developer, fitness instructor, marketer, and mother of five.

Visit her website at:
http://www.storytellingpower.com.

How to be a Storyteller With Senior Citizens

Author: Carol Esterreicher

Stories are enchanting and entrancing. When the novice or experienced storyteller begins, "Long ago, in a faraway country. . ." we are transported to another realm where "magic" is possible. Senior citizens (seniors) enjoy reminiscing and still appreciate experiencing the long ago and the far away again and again. Rather than restrict storytelling to mature or sober topics, plunge courageously into your favorite stories and test the waters. When you demonstrate a genuine interest in your senior audience, they truly appreciate the treasures you share with them.

Finding Senior Audiences

Organizations and social clubs typically invite guest speakers and entertainers to enhance their meetings and attract new members. Seniors populate these adult audiences. Your local Chamber of Commerce can help you to connect with groups and their contact persons. Your local government may publish lists of senior centers where active seniors teach classes, attend classes, enjoy social activities, and gather for lunch. These lists include names and phone numbers to facilitate contacting persons who can meet with you and discuss entertainment programs. County or local offices of Aging Services also lists independent-living residences, assisted-living residences, and rehabilitation hospitals. Explore Veterans Administration rehabilitation settings and discuss your proposed programs. Introduce your storytelling programs in person. Arrange to see the staff member or volunteer who schedules the programming at the senior setting you choose rather than just leaving your materials with someone who promises to deliver it to the intended person.

Reach out to your community. Participate in senior-center programs. When you are at the senior center, obtain a copy of the current month's programming schedule to learn what kinds of entertainment are already considered appropriate for the center's population. Ask if you might visit any of these events to become acquainted with the seniors and staff.

Request that your name be added to monthly newsletter mailing lists of senior centers and residential, independent and assisted-living centers. This will enable you to see throughout the seasons what to expect and what times of day, evenings, and weekend hours the entertainment is usually scheduled. When you get a sense of the programming routines, you can determine a place where storytelling adds the "flavor" you wish to provide. Your storytelling can enhance annual holiday celebrations and patriotic observances. For your nominal fee or other compensation, such participation can introduce you to staff and residents in various senior settings. Your introductory participation will ideally lead to invitations for more complete storytelling performances.

Remember that you can seek financial support from storytelling and performing arts organizations. In order to secure that first-time invitation in senior settings where the program managers are unfamiliar with storytelling, the process can be facilitated in several ways. When a storyteller can offer an introductory program at no cost, a welcoming and enthusiastic invitation can be obtained. *The National Storytelling*

Network annually invites individual project funding proposals. Arts organizations in your local area can be sources of funding that will assist your outreach to senior settings. Explore the possibilities!

Once your booking is confirmed, don't forget to publicize your upcoming event at the performance location. Use fliers and posters as needed. You can easily create these on your computer. Local newspapers often feature human-interest items. Read their articles until you identify a writer you feel motivated to approach regarding your program. The staff at the setting where you will be performing has, most likely, already made similar contacts and can recommend someone to you.

Discovering Stories for Senior Audiences

Tell your favorite stories and ask for suggestions! Provide paper and pencils and request written feedback. Eventually, you will perfect a streamlined way to obtain feedback to support storytelling in senior settings. Experiment with an easy form posing general questions, space for written comments, and optional requests for permission to quote. Draw attention to your request just before your concluding story. Complimentary quotes from seniors or staff can go a long way toward supporting storytelling programs. Consider attracting attention to the feedback forms and pencils by placing them near a bowl of individually-wrapped candies. I use the quotes on my website, as well.

Your form might include questions such as:

• "What did you like best about this storytelling program?"

• "What suggestions do you have?"

• "May I quote you in a storytelling publication or web site?"

From these completed evaluation forms, I have learned that seniors comment positively on storytelling programs featuring:

• Aesop's fables

• Classic fairy and folktales and tales told traditionally

• Fairy tales with word-play strategies such as
  spoonerisms

• Urban legends and superstitions

• Holiday and seasonal stories

• First-person portrayals (costumed or not) of prominent
  historical characters

• Characterizations of fictitious or real parents recalling
  family events

• Origins of selected holidays and celebrations

• Biographies of fine entertainers, authors, and some
  historical characters

• Parenthood and grandparenthood stories

• Humorous monologues, jokes, and anecdotes

The wide range of story types offers limitless opportunities to evoke sensory images—visual, auditory, tactile/kinesthetic, olfactory, gustatory and emotional/feeling responses. Intentional and skillful use of language, facial expressions, body language, and gestures evokes sensory images that make stories "come alive." Even though audiences of older seniors may be primarily women, remember to attend to the men in your audiences as well.

Here are some more ideas about gathering stories:

Sing-alongs are captivating! At a Florida Story Camp, a workshop presenter recommended engaging seniors in singing along to remembered "vintage" songs that have endured for generations. These songs have appeal with or without musical accompaniment. Patriotic songs, childhood camp songs, love songs and standard celebration songs like, "Take Me Out to the Ball Game," evoke memories and can set the stage for the story to come. Songs enhance the story already in progress or promote a memorable conclusion. Audiences are easily engaged in singing a song that embellishes a story well told. For example, they are most enthusiastic about singing, "She'll Be Comin' Around the Mountain When She Comes," as their singing becomes a part of the telling of historical railroad stories.

Consider engaging a musician friend or family member to provide musical accompaniment. With sufficient advance notice, perhaps a musically-inclined senior from your audience can be engaged to embellish a story and showcase his or her talent. You can find lyrics to songs from relevant decades on the Internet. If singing is not your preference, copies of poems and chants can be distributed as you encourage group participation. Remember to provide large-print resources!

Reminisce through holidays and seasonal observances. For example, one of my favorite stories to tell during the Christmas season is "The Chright Before

Nistmas." If you would like, you can listen to this story now at www.howtobeastoryteller.com/spoonerism.

Have fun with this story or one like it. Laughter is a beneficial and health-promoting experience!

Explore stories, songs, jokes, and riddles for your potential program content. Irish blessings, patriotism, world folklore, and historical events hold adult interest. Collect jokes and anecdotes your friends and relatives send you regarding aging and save them for just the right moment. Human beings are noted for making light of situations over which they have little control. Be sensitive to each audience while understanding that seniors themselves joke about aging. Exercising sensitivity, a storyteller can still entertain an aging audience with a humorous yet respectful perspective.

A young storyteller may choose to be more cautious using humor about aging. Senior storytellers who have some aging issues in common with older folks might be able to get away with poking more fun than their younger storytelling friends

Stories about parenting, grandparenting, and your own personal tales evoke memorable experiences we hold in common. They are potential themes for reflective storytelling programs with mature audiences. These magazines and websites with memories of daily life from decades ago can be helpful in creating good programs for seniors. The Internet has become a vast source of printable stories in practically any category that invites your curiosity.

Practical Tips for Telling to Senior Audiences

Be sure to ask, "Can you hear me?" We can trust that our elders like to listen to storytellers who make sure they can be heard! In some settings carpeting, draperies and upholstered chairs absorb sound. Even though you may be heard easily by those closest to you, the voice signal dissipates quickly. Some adults will speak up and let you know they are having difficulty hearing you. Others, not so vocal, will be quietly disappointed. Many centers will provide amplification if you ask.

A wireless microphone allows the storyteller to share hands-free presentations. A speaker placed in an optimal location at ear-level can assure comfortable listening for seniors and create a good speaking situation for the storyteller. Some seniors in the audience need hearing amplification and others will be wearing hearing aids that vary in sensitivity. So, they will (usually) let you know when they need you to speak more loudly.

Be prepared to answer, "How do you do that?" Audience members will ask if it is difficult to memorize stories. Storytellers typically become so familiar with the characters and the plot sequence of the stories they tell so that memorization is really not required. Be flexible and be ready to adjust to the needs of each situation. Start with short stories with a few characters and simple plots. Among the storytellers I know, I've heard that it is best to visualize or "walk around in your story." When a storyteller is involved in the story and the characters, the plot progresses naturally without the need to memorize. An exception may be a story poem or an essay that is better read word-for-word than memorized. Memorizing can change the delivery of a beautiful story into a mechanical recitation. Most storytellers prefer to tell rather than read stories and audiences really do appreciate and applaud the personalized touch that invites a response.

Consider intergenerational storytelling projects. In one senior center that partners with a local elementary school, my storytelling program was successfully intergenerational. The visiting second-grade students enjoyed listening to Aesop's fables and participated as I prompted them. The adults present appreciated the children's enthusiasm. A local origami artist followed with paper-folding instructions and pre-folded examples of tortoises and hares. Second-graders sat with seniors at lunchroom tables as they all folded the shapes together. The event ended with ice-cream cones shared with all participants. Be assured that Aesop's fables are timeless and ageless!

Finally, remember that seniors once were children, teenagers, students, lovers, teachers, parents, and grandparents. Many thrived as homemakers or went to work every day for years and made significant contributions to their professions. They love to reminisce about times gone by and often sigh with relief as they relinquish most of those responsibilities and look forward to retirement as a "retreading" of sorts. So let your imagination enlighten you and test the appropriateness of stories you already tell to friends and relatives.

About the Author:

Carol Esterreicher, Ed.S. During a lifetime of telling and teaching stories and more than twenty years of pro storytelling, Carol's audiences of all ages have enjoyed a delicious, dazzling, and sensory-rich variety of classic tales, urban legends, holiday favorites, folktales of many countries and costumed character portrayals. Audiences easily resonate to her tender and funny personal tales and storytelling.

Enjoying a most inspiring retirement after a 32-year career as a Speech and Language Pathologist, author, and Educational Specialist, Carol rightfully claims to know what kinds of stories seniors appreciate. "The National Storytelling Network" has honored her with the prestigious 2011 Oracle Award.

Visit her website at:
http://www.carolstories.com.

"If you don't know the trees, you may be lost in the forest. If you don't know the stories you may be lost in life."
—Attributed to Siberian Elders

How to be a Storyteller
In a Courtroom Setting

Author: Leslie Slape

Hello, lawyers. I'm that newspaper reporter scribbling notes during court. The one you're usually trying to ignore.

A couple of years ago, after a jury delivered a verdict in a murder trial, the judge in the case saw me in the superior court clerk's office and stopped to chat. He knew I was a storyteller.

"I think attorneys should be required to learn storytelling as part of their training, don't you agree?" he said.

"Absolutely," I replied.

In the case we had just heard, the defense attorney delivered a closing statement that explained the law and why the jury should acquit the defendant.

The prosecutor, on the other hand, told a story.

When I left that courtroom after the jury began deliberations, I had a vivid picture of the murder in my mind. I had to refer to my notes to remember what the defense attorney's points were.

The defendant could very well have been acting in self-defense, as the defense attorney said. Both attorneys had good reputations and a great deal of trial experience. Both presented their cases thoroughly and well. If I had been on the jury and based my vote on the testimony at trial, I would have had a hard time deciding. But the prosecutor was a masterful storyteller. Using details from the testimony, he took us back through the night of the murder until we could see it before our eyes. He presented the story in linear fashion, step by essential step. He was no showboat. He just told the story clearly and simply. By the time the prosecutor finished his closing statement, the jury was his.

The verdict: guilty.

The best way to illustrate a point, to have it lodge in the minds of the audience, is through story and storytelling.

Here's a brief overview of how storytellers work along with suggestions for adapting these techniques for your closing statement:

1. The Bones.

Storytellers learn a story by first identifying the "bones." Just like a skeleton that supports a body, the storytelling "bones" are all the essential points of the story. For example, the story of one famous version of "Little Red Riding Hood" might be broken into bones like this:

•Red's grandma is sick

•Mom gives basket to Red and warns don't talk to strangers

•Red meets wolf in woods and tells him where she's going

•Wolf takes shortcut to grandma's house

•He eats grandma

•He disguises himself as grandma

•He fools Red and eats her

Before telling the LRRH story, I run down those bones in my mind. That's all I need in order to remember it. Note that a story is best told in linear fashion. Flashbacks don't work well when information is transmitted orally.

An attorney's closing statement, told in story fashion, should be built the same way. I am not saying that you should not refer to your notes during your closing statement. If you know the bones, you will structure your argument around them, and the essential points will stick in the minds of the jury.

2. The Flesh.

Storytellers then put flesh on the bones by adding details that are essential to the message. It's just as important to exclude extraneous detail that could detract from the message.

Jurors are presented with a wealth of information in a trial, but if the closing statement includes only the essential details and is not a rehash of every detail, the attorney's message is clear and the jury is energized rather than exhausted.

3. The Words.

Storytellers use strong, clear, vivid words. Nouns and verbs are the most important. They employ adjectives and adverbs sparingly for maximum impact. Lawyers should do the same. When possible, with the jury as your audience, please avoid legalese.

4. The Presentation.

Storytellers are open-hearted. They make a direct connection with the audience. Listeners should feel as if the teller is speaking right to them. A story should feel, to the listener, as if it's true even if it's not. Storytellers aren't actors. I believe that when a storyteller presents a story in theatrical style, the audience loses interest. The teller no longer seems to have a personal connection with them. In the same way, lawyers should not be actors. If the story the lawyer is telling doesn't feel true, the jury won't believe it.

5. The Message.

The essential bones, proper amount of flesh, good word choice and clear, honest presentation will make the story's message obvious. The audience cannot fail to understand it. There's not even a need to add, "and the moral of the story is ..." An attorney who delivers a clear message might want to repeat it for emphasis, but there is no need to hammer away at the message.

After the trial that I mentioned above, the attorney left town for greener pastures. Since then, I've never seen an attorney use storytelling like that. A few do try, but they're in unfamiliar territory. Some load their stories with so much detail that the message is lost. Realizing this, they try to make their message clear by hammering at it, which always feels like desperation to me.

I don't claim to understand the law in depth. You attorneys are my masters there. However, I understand storytelling. Time and again I have seen that the best way to educate someone of any age, the best way to fix information in a person's mind, the best way to illustrate a point, is through story.

About the Author:

Leslie Slape fell in love with storytelling and folklore as a little girl.

In one way or another she has been telling stories all her life. In addition to telling professionally, she is also a playwright and theatrical stage manager and director. By day, she works as a newspaper journalist. She lives in Oregon with her husband, Max, on the farm where they raised their two now-grown children.

Learn more about her work at:
http://www.storyteller.net/tellers/lslape.

"Either write something worth reading or do something worth writing."
-Benjamin Franklin

How to be a Storyteller At a Story Slam

Author: Mark Goldman

Story Slams are taking the country by storm. A Story Slam is an open-mic (microphone) contest where people's names are drawn from a hat and then, in succession, they tell a true, personal story in five minutes, based on the night's theme. There are no notes, no props, no music, no costumes; just story, told in the oral tradition.

Generally credited as being the originator of the Slam model, "The Moth" was started in 1997 by George Dawes Green in New York City. Having moved from Georgia, he longed for the experience of telling stories on his grandmother's porch, where the moths would flutter around the porch light. What began as a small gathering in his apartment grew to enormous proportions in venues where people now line up around the block to get in.

The phenomenon has repeated itself in cities all across America and now in other countries too. Chicago, Los Angeles, San Francisco, Detroit, Pittsburgh and many other cities have Moth chapters. In addition, there are now many independent Story Slams all over, including the "Windy City Story Slam" in Chicago, "The Great Arizona Story Slam" in Phoenix and one of the most well-known, "Massmouth" in Massachusetts.

Winners of these contests are chosen in a variety of ways. Some have designated judges while some pick judges from the night's audience. The judges usually have criteria for scoring, based on how well the story was crafted, how well it was told and how well it adhered to the theme. Some Slams merely have audience applause at the end of the night to determine a winner. Prizes can vary from mere "bragging rights" to cash prizes to Massmouth's "MouthOff" grand prize of a week in Italy!

The elements of storytelling for a Slam are similar to telling in other venues and situations, but there are several additional fundamentals that should be considered. Let's take a look at everything that's involved.

It would seem that the most logical place to start would be to choose what story you will tell. But wait! Before you make your story choice, you must understand three important elements:

Element One: Know the Judging Process

Will this Slam use designated judges? If so, are they seasoned tellers themselves? Are they celebrity judges who may or may not understand story structure? Have they judged before? Do they have "favorite tellers" they like? Do they lean toward a particular style of telling? Are you aware of any other "quirks" a particular judge may have? Some judges take off points for sentimentality, sexually explicit or prurient material, angry "rants" or other personal dislikes. It should be noted that some Slams are designed to be sexually focused, like the Bay Area's "Bawdy Storytelling." I won't delve into any specifics here for these "fringe" type Slams, but I believe that similar criteria described in this chapter apply. Be sure you know what you are doing, storyteller!

These factors can all have an effect on how the judges make their evaluations, and ultimately what story and in what style you choose to tell. Whether judges are designated or randomly chosen from the audience, here is one set of typical rules that Slams follow. Make sure you check the specific rules of your particular Slam.

• Tell real stories. All stories must be true, personal stories.

• Retelling of any folktale, myth or fable, literary work or someone else's tale is not permitted.

• Don't use additional aids. The storyteller may not use written notes, props, costumes, or musical instruments.

• No poems are allowed unless the poem is original and tells a true story about you.

• Stay to the theme. Your entire story and not just the title or last line should connect in a meaningful way to the \ event's theme.

• Obey the time limit – "X" minutes means "X" minutes. There is usually a 60-second grace period to wind up. Going over the time limit may disqualify the teller or result in a loss of points.

There are judging rules, too. Each story is judged on:

• How well it is crafted.

• How well it is told.

• How well the story explores, connects and reveals some truth about the theme.

• There may be additional rules such as how well the teller connected to the audience.

Make sure you check for any additional or different rules for your Slam. Many Slams ask the judges to rate your storytelling based on the above criteria and award a "score" of 1-5 or 1-10 points for each category. Or they may just give one numerical score based on the cumulative criteria. Some Slams throw out the top and bottom scores and then average the remaining numbers. This often happens if the event is using five or more judges.

Element Two: Know Your Audience

Knowing your audience is crucial. Whether at a Slam, street performance, telling to a single person, 20 young children, or 300 adults in a tent or auditorium, understanding what it is that they want and what types of stories they will relate to is the single most important element of any successful storytelling event, including a Slam.

The other most common way of choosing a winner is a straight audience vote by applause. If this is the case, make sure you know your audience and what they like and want. What is the median age of the audience? What are the demographics? Is this a family crowd, or a rowdy group of Generation X-ers? Telling the "wrong" type of story can bury you, while telling a story that the audience is ready and waiting to hear can put you on the fast track to winning. And if your goal is winning in this type of audience-participation evaluation, you may want to consider bringing your own audience. Some may not consider this tactic "kosher," but be aware that many tellers employ this approach of "seeding" the audience.

Element Three: Know Your Theme

What is the theme for the Slam? Is it clearly defined? Is it loose and open to wide interpretation? The closer you can hone in on the essence of the theme, and craft a story that connects with that theme, the better your experience in telling your story and possibly winning.

Let me give you an example. If the theme is "A chance encounter with love," this is open to wide interpretation. It could be about a blind date, meeting your spouse for the first time (or the second time), a crush on a teacher or other stories about relationships between people. Now, think outside the box. It could also be about the first time you had a chocolate soufflé or maybe the time you found a stray dog in the park. It could be when it you saw a painting by Renoir. Perhaps you were stranded for a day in a strange city, and fell in love with the place, or even a small bookstore you discovered. It might be the love of a person, place, thing, yourself; an idea or philosophy. There are a myriad number of stories and plot lines that could fit that theme. A clever twist on the theme can be the ticket to success, but make sure you connect with the theme in some way, and the more ways, the better.

Now, based on your knowledge of the judges, the audience and the theme, it's time to decide what you will tell. The first rule: Make sure it is a true story about something that happened to you. There is no getting away from this. If it's not true, if it isn't your story, don't tell it! Know that if it's not a true, personal story, people will either know or eventually find out. And that spells disaster for you! So, follow the rules, and as my mother used to say, "Play nice."

Scour your mind and memories for all the stories that fit the theme of the Slam. Is there one that stands out for you? Is there one that you have told before? Is there one that you can tell in the designated time frame? Maybe there are several incidents or anecdotes that relate to the theme. You may want to find a way to connect them together in one coherent narrative. Remember, it doesn't have to be one story about one time in your life. You could use the device: "The first time I had a chance encounter with love was. . . My next chance encounter was. . . The last time I had a chance encounter with love was. . ."

Truth vs. Fact

"Was that a true story?" This is an age-old question, not just at the Story Slams, but also for any narrative presented as a personal story. Often, we use the words "truth" and "fact" to mean the same thing. In reality, they are a bit different. Understanding this distinction can help us in crafting true stories.

A "fact" is an occurrence that cannot be disputed. There is no emotion or feeling connected with a fact. It either is or is not a fact. Truth is more subjective. Truth is specifically personal to each of us. It is often how we experience or feel about things. At your family reunion, many things happened. Each of the relatives experienced them in different ways, and will relate "what happened" with a different story. Each story will be true.

Your story should contain your truth; how you experienced the events. Do not manufacture an incident, event or occurrence that did not happen.

Craft Your Story

In crafting your story, keep in mind all that you know about the judges and the audience. Make sure your story is crafted in a way that we can relate to what is going on. Translating personal incidents into universal experiences and feelings is essential. Find a way to make us care about what is happening in your story. Use foreshadowing, tension and release, irony, and other devices that will evoke engagement from the audience. Make us a promise that the story is going somewhere, and then make sure you deliver on that promise and take us there.

Don't leave out the humor in the story; just don't make it a "stand-up" routine. A good balance of humor and pathos can win the day. The best stories are the ones that bring us from laughter to tears and back again.

Don't forget the old maxim, "Show, don't tell." The great writer Anton Chekhov said, "Don't tell me the moon is shining, show me the glint of light on the broken glass."

Practice (And Coaching) Makes Perfect

Now comes one of the most crucial parts of telling for a Slam — practicing or rehearsing. Practice is essential in all storytelling, but even more so in a Slam. Why? Because it's a CONTEST! Don't ever forget that. If you want to win, consider it like you would a race or a sporting event. Great athletes practice every day. They warm up, they prepare; they push themselves to their limits so that when they perform in the actual event they will be at their peak. Their muscle-memory will be ingrained. Olympic athletes train for years, often for just a few seconds in the challenge. Storytellers would do well to take note.

You may find in your practice that you will want or need to change your story in some way: change your language; your tone; your pace; your facial expression or gestures, etc. Practicing is the way you hone your story to its finest and sharpest edge. Videotaping and watching yourself may be difficult, but it can make you aware of things you could never see, even by watching yourself in the mirror.

And like the athlete, it is always helpful to use a coach. A coach can see or hear things that you cannot. A good coach can push you to be your best in a way that you cannot do by yourself.
Timing is EVERYTHING!

Make sure you know what the time limit is BEFORE you start crafting your story. Find the time limit in PRINT (to be sure) somewhere in the Slam material. Find out if there is a "grace" period. If the limit is five minutes, do they signal you to wrap up within one more minute? Do you really have six minutes? Be absolutely clear about what the time frame, protocols and limits are!

Let me say it again, timing is everything! Know the Slam's time limit. Even more important, know the length of your story. Every time you practice your story, time it, start to finish, straight through. It helps if you know the time of each section. Try telling a little slower, pausing a bit more. Time it. Try telling a bit faster, pick up your pace. Time it. Settle on the best pace for your story and telling. Time it. Remember, you may also need to add some time in for audience reactions. There is no penalty for ending early. You will be better off if you end 30 seconds early than ONE second beyond the limit. One second too long and you will be disqualified.

Know where the timekeeper is sitting. If the producer has not told you who they are and where they are sitting, ASK! Do not leave this up to chance. Then, keep your eye on them. This is usually the person who holds up a sign, their hand, or stands at a specific time interval. Know the protocol. If you miss their signal and go over, it's your fault, not theirs. You will get nowhere by arguing or complaining. There's no crying in Slam telling. Sometimes, I like to have a friend sit right in front with a digital timer, like my cell phone, that I can see. That way, I can constantly monitor my time.

Here is my final admonition. Remember that few things in this world are absolute or guaranteed. You can do all the things I have suggested. You can craft a great story. You can target your audience and the judges. You can practice until you can tell your story in your sleep. Each piece of your telling can be exquisite and you can still lose. Fame is fleeting, and Story Slams are fickle. You never know who else will be telling and how their story will affect the audience and the judging. If you win, fantastic! If you don't win, graciously accept the fact that today was not your day. Remember that there is always a next time!

About the Author:

With a background in theater since the age of eleven, Mark Goldman has had an extremely eclectic life. He has been (in no particular order) an actor, director, stage manager, a speaking coach, magician, mediator, psychodrama therapist, web designer, meeting planner, and chef at a small New York City restaurant and bar.

Mark made a decision in January of 2011 to quit his job and focus full-time on storytelling. Along with telling to adults and children, he provides many outlets for local storytellers in Phoenix, Arizona by producing "S'More Stories Campfire Stories," a monthly storytellers' open-mic event as well as "The Great Arizona Story Slam."

Mark also publishes a weekly, online newsletter with storytelling tips and tidbits, and news about storytelling in Arizona. He recently joined the staff of "National Storytelling Network's" *Storytelling Magazine* as their advertising representative.

Find his website at:
http://www.storytellermark.com.

How to be a Storyteller Across Language Barriers

Author: Dr. Wajuppa Tossa

"You have become quite a storyteller."

That was Dr. Margaret Read MacDonald's comment after my first storytelling tour in the United States in 1996 with four students in my storytelling project, set up to engender pride in local cultural heritage among young people in northeast Thailand. That was the proudest moment and the day I decided to be a storyteller.

My becoming a storyteller actually is due to two major factors. Those being a simultaneous translator for lectures and storytelling performances and learning to tell stories with a master storyteller as a mentor. I am grateful to have a chance to work with Dr. MacDonald as my mentor in the "Storytelling Project."

At the onset of the project, Dr. MacDonald joined my project as a Fulbright visiting scholar in 1995, helping me to teach university students to collect, select, and adapt folktales for storytelling performances. There was a serious problem at the beginning because Dr. MacDonald did not speak much Thai and the students that joined my project did not have a good enough command of English to listen to lectures or stories in English. So Dr. MacDonald suggested that I translate her lectures in Lao, one of the major dialects in northeast Thailand. When she taught storytelling techniques and told stories as models for students to learn to retell, I also

97

translated into Lao. Actually the official language in Thailand is central Thai and it is required that everyone speak it in formal and official settings.

When I used the dialect, it was contrary to my expectations. Students became very excited. The nature of the spoken Lao is earnest and down-to-earth and very fun to listen to. Thus, it was very effective. At that time I did not consider myself a storyteller. I was the translator. But because I had known Dr. MacDonald quite well before she came to join my project, I felt very comfortable working with her. I felt so comfortable that when I made a mistake, I could ask her to go back to the part that I mistranslated and then I could translate it correctly. This happened a lot because most of the stories that Dr. MacDonald told as models were unknown to me and the translation was simultaneous.

For example, one time, Dr. MacDonald was telling "Lifting the Sky" by Vi Hubert. The sky was so low that people kept bumping their heads against the sky and some people went to play in the skyworld when it was not the right time. So the chiefs came together to decide what to do. I misheard the word "chiefs" as "sheeps." So I translated that all the sheep came together to make long poles to push up the sky. When the story came to the part when they were pushing up the sky with the long poles, I realized that it was "chiefs" not "sheeps." So, I apologized and asked her to regress. Everyone just thought it was funny. My making mistakes in translation was not at all bad because it made my students feel comfortable to learn and that mistakes could happen. They became less intimidated. Of course, the mistakes were not intentional, but it gave a good effect in the long run.

The second factor that enabled me to become a good storyteller was to learn from the real master storyteller. While translating I would observe how she told and how she engaged the audience while telling. When I translated her stories, I tried to capture the emotional expressions from her telling and tried to add those expressions in my Lao versions of the stories. It worked out very well. After telling stories with her so often, I picked up a lot of tips in telling. We even developed a very good rhythm and pace in telling together. It has become a new tandem telling, in two languages. When she went to tell stories with her friends from other countries, like Japan, Indonesia, Cuba, Argentina, and so on, she used the same techniques. Now this type of tandem telling is popular among storytellers in international storytelling festivals where English is not the language of the audience.

I have had chances to tell in international storytelling festivals where I was assigned to tell stories with a translator such as in Indonesia and in Iran. When that happened, I adapted the techniques I learned from Dr. MacDonald. First, I would get to know the translator. I would gather information about the translator from our informal communications. I would learn about what the person was like and what he or she liked or disliked. Afterward, we would share stories that are more personal. Once we got to know each other well enough and once we liked each other, the storytelling in tandem went well. Most of the time, the translators were not storytellers. They would just translate into their languages. I then asked the translators to add voices, facial expressions, and gestures in the translations.

That process worked well when I did that in Iran the first time. My translator was a teacher and was older and quite well-respected. She was able to convince the committee to allow her to be expressive in her translation. In my second telling in Iran, I had a young translator who was still a university student. It was hard for her to convince the committee to allow movements and facial expressions in her translation. It was forbidden for girls to be expressive in public in Iran. However, my translator did very well in using her tones of voice, the loudness and softness in pronouncing each word appropriately. Thus, the storytelling was successful. The tip in tandem telling in two languages here would be to get to know the translator personally first and then work with him or her on the tips of how to be successful in storytelling performances.

When I told stories in Indonesia, most translators were storytellers as well so it was not difficult to make tandem telling in two languages work. However, I found that when I was able to use the Bahasa Indonesian words in my telling, it was very well received. As a lover of various languages, I always try to learn new words or sentences in other languages when I have opportunities. So, when I told stories in Indonesia, I learned a few words. When I told stories, I would add those local words in my telling. When I did that the audience was very happy. So, the suggestion here is for storytellers to learn some words in local languages and use them in their telling. If there is no opportunity to learn these words beforehand, the storytellers need to be quick and remember words that the translators use, like songs or refrains.

Finally, when we are in a situation when the translator is unable to work, what should we do to tell stories to the audience who does not know the language? I have a suggestion for this case. I was in a situation when I could not speak at all. I had laryngitis when I was going to tell stories in Vientiane, Laos once. I did not know what to do. So, I used finger stories and stories with a lot of gestures, clear gestures, like "Two Goats on the Bridge." My students were able to help with voices, but these types of stories work. In some situations, I used the techniques of asking the audience to do and say what I do or say. This kind of story is usually short with simple structures along with many repetitions. By the time we finish telling the story, the audience will be able to retell the story on their own. My best suggestion here would be to simplify the language and structures of the stories to make them useful for telling in a setting where there is no translator.

In conclusion, my advice to storytellers across language barriers would be the following: first to get to know the translator well, second, to be observant, to learn some words or phrases to use, and to use voices, facial expressions, and gestures in telling. With all or some of these, language is no longer a barrier and the storytelling will be successful.

About the Author:

Associate Professor Dr. Wajuppa Tossa, B.Ed. (English) and M.Ed. (English Language and Literature) from Srinakharinwirot University, Prasanmitra, Ph.D. (English and American Literature) from Drew University, Madison, New Jersey, USA, teaches at Mahasarakham University Thailand since 1978. She tells stories to revitalize Thai/Lao folktales and storytelling tradition. She has performed and given workshops on folktales and storytelling in USA, Australia, Singapore, and Indonesia. Wajuppa's books include Phadaeng Nang Ai and "Phya Khankhaak, the Toad King" (1990,1996), "Lao Folktales" (2008) and parts of "Telling Tales of Southeast Asia and Korea" (2011).

How to be a Storyteller Developing Great Characters

Author: Leeny Del Seamonds

How do you bring stories to life? When spoken word is brought to life, several performance skills and techniques come into play: incorporating healthy phonation and compelling vocal variety, "standing in your setting," applying motivated actions and gestures, and developing palpable story characters.

As performers, we often portray multiple characters in stories. However, we don't want each of our characters to look and sound the same. We want them to be distinctive, individual and believable. To achieve this, it's essential to research, interpret and develop distinguished, well-defined and clear-cut story characters by approaching each character as an actor would approach researching and developing a character in a play. Having an appropriate voice for each character is fundamental. The whole body plays a part in obtaining and maintaining healthy phonation (a fit, strong voice); in creating diverse vocal pitches and qualities; and in crafting vivid, precise character voices. We use our bodies, hands and faces to enhance communication and frequently add gestures, movement and/or mime along with vocal variety to portray convincing characterizations. Determining the story character's personality, motivation, physical characteristics, and how she moves and sounds are all part of "breathing life" into story characters.

There are "3 R's" of character development: research, rehearse and refine.

We will start with the first "R": Research.

Whether you are adapting a folk tale or writing a family/personal story, research plays an important role in character creation and story setting. Conducting research requires good detective skills and a well-developed sense of curiosity. When researching – and ultimately performing – a multicultural tale, one of my goals is to accurately replicate a character's accent and gestures, while incorporating a selection of the foreign language into the story, thus maintaining cultural authenticity and avoiding stereotypical caricatures of members of foreign cultures. When writing a personal story, research is equally key in accurately portraying believable characters. These might include relatives, ancestors, real people and fictional personas.

The following resources may prove helpful with research: libraries, museums, anthologies, folklore collections, reference books, abundant web sites on the Internet designed for storytelling research, movies from a particular era or country, maps and atlases, history and social studies books, computer CDs, DVDs, magazines, and interviewing people (including relatives) from a specific country/culture. This is a personal favorite, but you may think of additional resources to gain knowledge and facts pertaining to your story and its characters.

Before analyzing and interpreting your story character, think about some of the following:

1. What is the geographical location, the date, year, season, climate, and time of day?

2. What is the economic, social, religious and political environment?

3. Where is the setting? Setting is usually significant to your story, especially when creating unique, clear story characters. If this information doesn't exist in the traditional tale, adapt it by creating your own setting using various resources to make accurate decisions.

Let's take a look at character analysis, traits and personality. Every performer should answer three questions about each character that they will portray:

1. Who am I? Define the character's personality traits, appearance, age, voice, and unusual features/qualities.

2. What do I want? Determine the character's goals and their objectives.

3. What am I willing to do to get it? How does the character attempt to achieve these goals? What is the character's motivation for doing what she does?

Make a list of adjectives to describe each character. Include personality, temperament, physical characteristics, abilities and/or limitations. Contemplate what others might say about that character. Is there a fatal flaw which is the character's undoing (such as greed, lust, vanity, jealousy, desperation)? Find at least one redeeming quality about each character, one with which you can identify and ultimately justify why this character is the way she is.

Think about dialogue in the story. What does the character say or think aloud? Consider choice of words used by the character and her style or manner of speaking. Does the character have a dialect? If so, research authentic accents by listening to foreign language tapes or audio recordings by natives from a particular culture. Watch movies from a foreign country, especially ones which feature an actor with a foreign accent. Interview someone from a specific culture/foreign country and record accents, tempo and speech patterns.

Consider the previous action of the character. What happened to this character before entering the first scene of the story and what action involving the character occurs between scenes? Look carefully at the initial mood/intensity of each character at the beginning of the story. Determine where this character was before the story begins and what they were doing. Does this character change and/or grow during the course of the story? If so, in what ways?

You will also need to "find the voice" of your character. What is the sound of your character? Think about vocal pitch, dynamics, tempo, quality.

Experiment with various voices to find the best one to suit your character. To create well-inflected and expressive voices, be aware of:

1. Pitch and Range- the intervals of sound tones, from high to low.

2. Dynamics- the volume of sound, loud to soft.

3. Tempo- the speed and rhythm of sound.

4. Articulation- your diction and clear delivery.

A digital recorder is a valuable tool to help hear the differences in voice selection and aids in identifying one character voice from another. A full-length mirror is useful in seeing what the character looks like as you test various gestures, body positions, facial expressions, etc. Be aware of your hands when speaking – try not to repeat the same hand gesture or use a repetitive hand pattern. Watch yourself in the mirror or ask a trusted friend/coach to observe you.

In developing more than one story character, use the character analysis research to compare and contrast qualities and personality traits of each one. Experiment with diverse interpretations of voice and body stance/position, making each character exclusive, exceptional and distinct.

Now it is time for the second "R": Rehearse.

I am a firm believer in creating hard copies of my stories. It is highly beneficial to write or type your stories-in-progress because these writings become your scripts. Use your script to rehearse, make changes, keep notes and include introductions. Be prepared to edit your script several times, incorporating changes as you practice the story aloud. Recording your stories in this early writing and rehearsal period and listening to them while following the scripts and making necessary changes is useful and recommended.

The script also becomes your reference point every time you go back to the story for review or additional work. The script is a good place to keep notes such as the length of story (running time), specific intros, actions and movements and voice comments.

Read your story script aloud over and over until you become extremely familiar with it. It's a good idea to memorize any dialogue so the words flow easily and believably from your characters. Work with a pencil and mark changes so you can incorporate them when editing the script. Typing your script on a computer is advisable because it cuts down on rewriting and editing time. There are differences between a written story and oral storytelling. Write your story to be heard and not to be read. As you type, speak the words aloud in your style of telling.

Once you have created a good working script, you can begin the process of blocking your story. "Blocking" is a theater term which means "adding movement to the script." Even if you choose not to have much movement in your story with action, gestures and body motions, you should still determine several factors. What body position/stance does each character have when conversing? What gestures do you wish to use to "paint word pictures?" If you want to incorporate actions into your storytelling, which actions (such as running in place, climbing or sword fighting) do you plan to portray?

Above all, decide where and how you will stand in your story. It's essential to immerse yourself in the story and be in the moment while telling the tale. One way to do this is to "stand in your setting." Using imagination and the research you've conducted to create the setting, place yourself in the middle of the village, jungle, kingdom, prairie, marketplace, kitchen, forest, villa or desert of your tale. As the narrator in your story, determine where you are standing; and when you look around, you should "see" all the surroundings (buildings, trees, streams, animals, people and so forth) that your setting encompasses. Additionally, decide from which direction each character enters and exits a scene in the story. In most cases, the narrator would gesture to that location when introducing the character and may watch that character leave the scene.

As narrator, when introducing an object or character to the audience, you must totally believe that the object or character exists. If you look at the character or use mime to pick up an object, the audience sees it too. In many ways, the object or character becomes as real to the audience as it is to the storyteller. Seeing is believing. In mime training, this is the first thing we are taught. If we create it, it becomes real. There also should be the same level of motivated believability in the actions and gestures we portray.

Practice, Practice, Practice! Once you are ready to tell your story aloud, practice it over and over again, making necessary edits. You don't need to memorize your script, although you should be extremely familiar with it. I do suggest you memorize the dialogue, that is, what your characters say. Again, recording your story is very useful in learning it and helps to determine the story's timing. As you develop programs, you will want to know how much time it takes to tell your story. To help with practice, I use my digital recorder to record the stories. I then transfer them to the computer and burn a CD so I can listen to the stories and learn them in the car.

Here's the final "R": Refine.

The job of refining, or polishing, your story may seem like a never-ending process. You probably will experiment with, and make changes to, your story numerous times. Practice "jumping" (switching) from one speaking character to another, keeping your characterizations distinct and clear. Making clean, crisp delineation between narrator and characters helps to breathe life into the story and keep it tight.

Practice telling the story as often as you can to someone you trust, to a small group of listeners, to another storyteller or coach. Ask for honest, constructive feedback, especially on your character interpretations. Do your story characters differ from one another? How would your listeners describe them? Is there any part of the story that doesn't make sense? Can they hear and understand you? Does the story flow? Listen carefully to feedback and suggestion and write down the changes you wish to incorporate in your script.

Keep files of your scripts (with edits) and include various introductions (lead ins) for each story, since one story could be introduced in several different ways during more than one season. I keep the running time of each story circled at the top left-hand corner of the script for quick reference when putting together a specific program and need an idea of the total length of the show.

In closing, I'd like to share my "Words of Wisdom" to storytellers: Be true to you. Don't imitate anyone else's style. Write and perform your own stories, original or adapted, with your personality using words you normally use. Be as honest as you can, allowing the audience to see the real you. Be yourself, respecting your presence with each audience.

"¡Vive el Cuento! Live the Story!"

About the Author:

Leeny Del Seamonds, *Master Story Performer*™, is a multi award-winning, internationally acclaimed performer of Latino, original and World tales spiced with mime, palpable characterizations, and love of people. A dedicated Teaching Artist with a BA in Theatre/Performing Arts (magna cum laude), Leeny encourages listeners to rejoice in cultural diversity, inviting them to share in her Cuban-American sense of humor and joy of performing. With passion, fire and wit, Leeny's celebrated one-woman performances and renowned workshops headline events worldwide.

You can find her website at:
http://leenydelseamonds.com.

"Go beyond the words."

How to be a Storyteller Using Advanced Techniques

Author: Kathy Jessup

So you've found a story. It is a really good story and you have worked hard to learn it forwards and backwards and inside out. You can tell it straight through without forgetting anything, and you've even practiced how to keep your voice expressive and interesting. Has the time come when you can finally tell it to an audience? Well---almost.

Beyond The Words

Go beyond the words. Think of this process as painting first with a broad brush and then going over your work with a fine liner to put in the detail. Once the basics of your story are set in your head, you can concentrate on the little things that truly make or break the telling of a tale. Here below are a few of these things to consider.

1. Pacing

It is common for people to increase their rate of speech when nervous or to rush a story's ending. Like a horse heading for the barn, your temptation is to speed up when you know the end is in sight. Be conscious of this and try to make sure your story is delivered with a consistent pacing, neither rushed nor too slow. The exception, of course, is when you deliberately speed up or slow down for a particular section of a story to give it an emotional twist.

2. Mannerisms and Gestures

My distinction between these two is that mannerisms are habitual movements you make without thinking, while gestures are something you deliberately add to your storytelling. Both run the risk of being distracting if not kept under control. Mannerisms can be a result of nervousness and might include twirling your hair, fidgeting, tapping your leg, jingling the change in your pocket, rocking or pacing. If someone brings it to our attention, we're often amazed, saying something like "Do I really do that? I didn't know!" You'll need to work on eliminating repetitive mannerisms as they can definitely be a distraction for your audience.

Gestures, on the other hand, are one of a storyteller's tools for livening up the delivery of a story. Some tellers have a more subdued style and use very few gestures. Often I find these tellers have a particularly expressive storytelling voice which helps keep the listener spellbound. Don't mistake a lack of gestures for rigidity. These tellers keep their bodies relaxed and open, so that even the slightest movement adds nuance to the story. The other extreme is an over-use of gestures, or gestures that seem demonstratively louder (broader) than necessary. Constant movement may be annoying to some listeners, and detracts from the gestures that truly add something to your story. Give careful thought to where you place gestures, what your options are for movement and how big the gestures need to be. A large, expansive arm swing can seem "in your face" within the context of a small story circle, but be perfectly in tune with a larger stage performance.

3. Eye Contact

This is very tricky! When we are nervous (as beginning tellers often are), our inclination is to avoid eye contact. Yet deep down we know just how important it is to look someone in the eye when you're talking to them. Storytelling creates a relationship between Teller and Listener. Audience members need to feel a connection to you and that begins with eye contact. The best advice is to watch experienced tellers perform. Note how their eyes roam casually as they tell, eventually including every part of the room, front row to back row and side to side. Of course, you always want your gaze to appear random and not follow a predictable pattern. You don't have to linger on a particular person for too long, so it shouldn't be awkward. Eye contact does get easier the more you practice it!

Taking Control On Stage

It is wise to remember that you are "on stage" from the moment the audience can see you, and your performance doesn't end until you disappear from sight. "Stage presence" means taking comfortable command of the stage from the moment you walk on. It is your space, so own it! With that in mind, it's worth discussing a few of the "nuts and bolts" that are critically important to a successful storytelling performance and yet really don't have anything to do with the actual story.

Nerves: There are many fine books out there to help you with relaxation exercises and stage fright issues. I firmly believe one of the best ways to control nerves is to eliminate nasty last-minute surprises at the venue. There is nothing worse than going on-stage "rattled" because you've been distracted by venue problems. Avoid disasters by having a detailed advance discussion with the person booking you and being clear about your requirements. If possible, check out the venue ahead of time or, better yet, catch the story set before yours so you can see and hear things for yourself. If something is not set up right, then change it so it meets your needs as a storyteller.

For example, if the stage is positioned in such a way that the sun is in your eyes, or there is a pillar blocking your sightlines, try altering where you stand. A few steps sideways might be enough to make a difference. If the acoustics are lousy, see if you can move the audience closer to you or you to them. If noise is still an issue, explain to organizers that you are a storyteller not a storyYELLER. Ask politely but firmly for other location options, or a microphone. Be confident that you are not being difficult. You are being professional.

Microphones: Bad microphones and poor microphone technique have sabotaged many a storytelling performance. If you are serious about becoming a storyteller, it is a good idea to learn how to use a microphone. You might start out telling in small groups, but sooner or later you'll find yourself in a situation where a microphone is necessary, so why wait to learn? Over the years, I've heard many storytellers insist "I don't need a microphone, I'm loud enough." Then, I've sat in the audience struggling to hear those very same tellers. Remember, a microphone isn't for you; it's for your audience. Why take the chance they'll miss hearing parts of your story?

I suspect that reluctance to use a microphone often stems from a teller's inexperience with handling one. That inexperience then translates into nervousness. It really doesn't cost much to rent a microphone kit for a weekend, and the opportunity to practice is invaluable.

There are several types of microphones for different sorts of venues and situations, and all have advantages and disadvantages. Once you are comfortable with the microphone it is one less thing to worry about while telling your story.

Entrance and Exit: Remember my earlier point about how you are "on stage" from the moment the audience can see you? When scoping out your venue ahead of time, it is very helpful to check your route to the stage. Is it one step up or a staircase? If lights are dimmed, will you be able to clearly see your path? Are there any cords in the way that might catch you up? These may seem like pesky details, but it is a teller's worse nightmare to trip their way into the spotlight!

I remember one particular concert where a teller had a mobility issue. The host introduced her, applause followed her name, and then there were several long moments while she laboriously made her way up the stairs (in full view of the audience) to the stage. Out of breath, she was then in no shape to begin telling her story. This was an awkward scene for both teller and audience. In hindsight, it was painfully obvious that with some considerate planning and foresight the situation could have been avoided.

Meanwhile, let's pretend you have confidently navigated your way to center stage and have just reached the microphone stand. The temptation is to immediately begin, but don't rush it! You have time. The audience is still adjusting to your presence, and you need time to do the same. Breathe. Settle your nerves and your posture. While doing so, take a couple of seconds to look out at the audience and soak in their introductory applause. Then you are ready to begin.

117

For every beginning there is an ending, and the way you exit the stage is just as important as your entrance. Here we come to what is perhaps one of the hardest things for any storyteller to learn: how to graciously accept applause. It is quite common to see a new storyteller quickly run off the stage the moment their last word is uttered. Head down, they are charging for the exit while the bewildered audience is still digesting the story's ending and hasn't even had the opportunity to begin clapping. We may loathe appearing conceited, but it is not conceit to take a moment and acknowledge the audience's gratitude. As painful as it may be, force yourself to stand there for at least a few seconds. Count silently if you have to, but give listeners an opportunity to show their thanks for the story and for your telling of it. If you still feel uncomfortable while basking in their applause, it may help to think about all of the work you put in to getting the story performance-ready. Surely that time and effort is worth a few seconds of applause?

All of these "Do's and Don'ts" can seem a bit overwhelming. Like any art form, storytelling takes practice and it is not something you can master quickly. Take comfort in knowing that, on a basic level, you already are a storyteller. You do it instinctively every day when you communicate with those around you. As you deepen your knowledge of storytelling techniques and repertoire, trust that your skills will grow. It is a ladder with many rungs and even experienced tellers are continually challenged. Tell stories because you love to tell stories. Tell often, in as many different places and circumstances as you can. Don't worry if your delivery isn't perfect; your audience isn't perfect either!

I have one final tip. This one may surprise you: begin by listening. Go to places where you can hear other storytellers, be it a concert, story circle, festival or living room. Buy or borrow storytelling recordings and videos. Your assignment: watch, listen, absorb, digest stories and storytelling. Then, it is time for you to tell. You have just been handed the best school assignment ever. Enjoy!

About the Author:

Kathy Jessup tells original stories and world folktales at schools, libraries, concerts and festivals across Canada. She has a special fondness for stories that make people laugh, and for tales that come from her Irish heritage. Kathy's original stories have been published in various literary venues and included on several cd anthologies. Her solo CD "Listen up! Tellable Tales for Hungry Ears" is recommended by the Canadian Children's Book Centre guide "Best Books for Kids and Teens."

Kathy shares her passion for storytelling with others through workshops, presentations and speaking engagements for a wide variety of organizations. She also loves to travel and has enjoyed numerous touring experiences that have taken her to some far-flung communities. She's swapped tales with Irish Tellers in Dublin, Ireland. She has entertained Inuit children in Canada's far north, and told ghost stories in a rural cemetery.

To learn more, you can visit Kathy's website at:
http://www.kathyjessup.com.

Other Helpful Resources

Our Storytelling 101 Eworkbook and coaching kit will be very helpful to you as you create stories. Filled with plenty of action steps, you will learn more about the process of crafting stories and the skills needed to present them to live audiences. You will also learn and practice methods to collect stories, anecdotes and floats from within your family or organization. The Ekit also comes with mp3 audio files and 30 minutes of telephone coaching with Sean Buvala. To learn more, please visit the website at: http://www.storytelling101.com.

Learn to take the smallest fragment of a story and turn it into a full tale. Pick up Sean Buvala's **"Measures of Story: How to Create a Story From Floats and Anecdotes."** You can read free training articles and learn more at: http://www.howtocreateastory.com.

Learn to be a hero to your kids and teach them your values (with storytelling) when you get the **"DaddyTeller"** parenting book. Step-by-step instructions and fun stories to share with your young children. Visit http://www.daddyteller.com

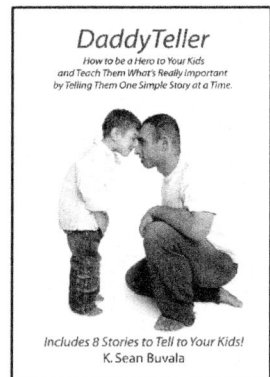

DaddyTeller

How to be a Hero to Your Kids
and Teach Them What's Really Important
by Telling Them One Simple Story at a Time.

Includes 8 Stories to Tell to Your Kids!
K. Sean Buvala

About Storyteller.net

This book project is a celebration of 15 years of service to the community. Fifteen years is "forever" in terms of the Internet. We are even older than that very famous search engine.

Starting in 1997, we were the first to offer a comprehensive online directory for storytellers. Hundreds of storytellers have used or are using our services and we are glad to have given them a home. We've watched tellers transition and grow from simple, beginning local tellers to some of the best nationally-travelled tellers in the business.

We were the first to offer a diverse collection of online audio stories, free for listening for audiences all over the world. There's also a growing collection of written stories on our site. We've had two editions of the Storyteller.net store, with our current store at StorytellingProducts.com going strong.

We were the first to offer the podcast-like *Amphitheater* with storytelling interviews and performances. Yes, we were doing "podcasts" before they even had a word to describe "podcasts." Little did we know that what we were doing was very far ahead of the Internet pack.

Please visit Storyteller.net and see what we have in store for you in the coming years.

Printed in Great Britain
by Amazon

83939238R00078